THE COMING ECONOMIC ARMAGEDDON

What Bible Prophecy Warns about the New Global Economy

D1260779

DR. DAVID JEREMIAH

with Dr. David Jeremiah

© 2010 by Turning Point for God
P.O. Box 3838
San Diego, CA 92163
All Rights Reserved

Edited by William Kruidenier
Unless otherwise indicated, Scripture verses quoted are from the NEW KING JAMES VERSION.

The financial statistics in this study guide were current at the time Dr. Jeremiah preached this series in the fall of 2009 and early 2010. Events may have caused data to change since that time.

Printed in the United States of America.

CONTENTS

ABOUT DR. DAVID JEREMIAH AND TURNING POINT

D r. David Jeremiah is the founder of Turning Point, a ministry committed to providing Christians with sound Bible teaching relevant to today's changing times through radio and television broadcasts, audio series, and books. Dr. Jeremiah's common-sense teaching on topics such as family, prayer, worship, angels, and biblical prophecy forms the foundation of Turning Point.

David and his wife, Donna, reside in El Cajon, California, where he serves as the senior pastor of Shadow Mountain Community Church. David and Donna have four children and ten grandchildren.

In 1982, Dr. Jeremiah brought the same solid teaching to San Diego television that he shares weekly with his congregation. Shortly thereafter, Turning Point expanded its ministry to radio. Dr. Jeremiah's inspiring messages can now be heard worldwide on radio and television, and the Internet.

Because Dr. Jeremiah desires to know his listening audience, he travels nationwide holding ministry rallies and spiritual enrichment conferences that touch the hearts and lives of many people. According to Dr. Jeremiah, "At some point in time, everyone reaches a turning point; and for every person, that moment is unique, an experience to hold onto forever. There's so much changing in today's world that sometimes it's difficult to choose the right path. Turning Point offers people an understanding of God's Word as well as the opportunity to make a difference in their lives."

Dr. Jeremiah has authored numerous books, including *Escape the Coming Night* (Revelation), *The Handwriting on the Wall* (Daniel), *Overcoming Loneliness, Grand Parenting, The Joy of Encouragement, Prayer—The Great Adventure, God in You* (Holy Spirit), *Gifts from God* (Parenting), *Jesus' Final Warning, When Your World Falls Apart, Slaying the Giants in Your Life, My Heart's Desire, Sanctuary, Life Wide Open, Searching for Heaven on Earth, The Secret of the Light, Captured by Grace, Discover Paradise, Grace Givers, Why the Nativity?, Signs of Life, The 12 Ways of Christmas, 1 Minute a Day, What in the World Is Going On?* and *Living With Confidence in a Chaotic World.*

ABOUT THIS
STUDY GUIDE

The purpose of this Turning Point study guide is to reinforce Dr. David Jeremiah's dynamic, in-depth teaching and to aid the reader in applying biblical truth to his or her daily life. This study guide is designed to be used in conjunction with Dr. Jeremiah's *The Coming Economic Armageddon* audio series, but it may also be used by itself for personal or group study.

STRUCTURE OF THE LESSONS

Each lesson is based on one of the messages in the *The Coming Economic Armageddon* compact disc series and focuses on specific passages in the Bible. Each lesson is composed of the following elements:

- *Outline*

The outline at the beginning of the lesson gives a clear, concise picture of the topic being studied and provides a helpful framework for readers as they listen to Dr. Jeremiah's teaching.

- *Overview*

The overview summarizes Dr. Jeremiah's teaching on the passage being studied in the lesson. Readers should refer to the Scripture passages in their own Bibles as they study the overview.

- *Application*

This section contains a variety of questions designed to help readers dig deeper into the lesson and the Scriptures, and to apply the lesson to their daily lives. For Bible study groups or Sunday school classes, these questions will provide a springboard for group discussion and interaction.

- *Did You Know?*

This section presents a fascinating fact, historical note, or insight that adds a point of interest to the preceding lesson.

Using This Guide for Group Study

The lessons in this study guide are suitable for Sunday school classes, small-group studies, elective Bible studies, or home Bible study groups. Each person in the group should have his or her own study guide.

When possible, the study guide should be used with the corresponding compact disc series. You may wish to assign the study guide as homework prior to the meeting of the group and then use the meeting time to listen to the CD and discuss the lesson.

For Continuing Study

For a complete listing of Dr. Jeremiah's materials for personal and group study call 1-800-947-1993, go online to www.DavidJeremiah.org, or write to: Turning Point, P.O. Box 3838, San Diego, CA 92163.

Dr. Jeremiah's *Turning Point* program is currently heard or viewed around the world on radio, television, and the Internet in English. *Momento Decisivo*, the Spanish translation of Dr. Jeremiah's messages, can be heard on radio in every Spanish speaking country in the world. The television broadcast is also broadcast by satellite throughout the Middle East with Arabic subtitles.

Contact Turning Point for radio and television program times and stations in your area. Or visit our website at www.DavidJeremiah.org.

THE COMING ECONOMIC ARMAGEDDON

INTRODUCTION

Every mother knows this about births: They are unpredictable; each one is different. There's another birth—the only one of its kind in history—that is coming due soon, and its timing will be unpredictable as well: the birth of the kingdom of God on earth. Jesus Christ is coming back to earth to establish His kingdom to rule and reign as King of Kings and Lord of Lords for one thousand years.

Even though we don't know exactly when the specific events leading up to the birth of the kingdom will take place—events like the Rapture of the Church, followed by the seven-year Tribulation —we will experience "birth pangs" that tell us the time is drawing near. Every mother knows "that feeling" that comes with the onset of labor, the pains that tell her the blessed event is drawing nigh. And it will be the same with the coming kingdom of God: pain and discomfort on a global scale—"groans and labors with birth pangs" (Romans 8:22).

The world began experiencing discomfort in a serious way in 2008—economic birth pangs causing unprecedented degrees of pain and suffering around the world. And as of the publishing of this study guide, the pains show no signs of letting up. Bad financial policy at many levels came to a head in the fall of 2008 and caused a collapse of confidence in the world's economic infrastructure. Those waves of upheaval have trickled down to the man and woman on the street—loss of jobs and income, evaporating savings, home foreclosures, and the revelation that financial institutions and authorities don't always operate with the best interests of the public in mind.

But there is another dimension of the crisis that discernment will discover. The steps taken by governments around the world to put a hedge around the growing financial chaos have created new forms of consolidation and control that will have ominous repercussions.

Governments have inflated their money supplies by printing massive amounts of currency—paper money with no backing—in order to rescue financial institutions and stimulate economies. They have incurred billions, in some cases trillions, of dollars of debt which stand no chance of being repaid. And at the same time they have extended their reach into the lives of private citizens—such as the healthcare entitlement mandated by the United States government.

All this government activity, set in motion either because of, or commensurate with the economic upheaval beginning in 2008, has resulted in increased calls for a "new world order" or a "new economic order"—a world-level structure that would put some kind of government body in charge of solving the problems faced by the global community. And because everything—food, clothing, shelter, jobs—is a function of finances, a combination "new world economic order" seems destined to emerge.

Students of biblical prophecy will not be caught off guard by these developments. As far back as the prophet Daniel, Scripture has foretold the rise of an end-time government led by the most despotic dictator in history. This leader will be "Satan's CEO," empowered by the devil to move people's eyes away from Christ and toward himself, the Antichrist. Because of his power, this leader will control who can buy and who can sell in the world. And people who are hungry will swear allegiance to him rather than starve.

The Coming Economic Armageddon has been written to help you understand what was foretold in the past, what is happening right now, and how to prepare for the future. But most of all, it has been prepared to encourage you to put your trust and hope in God—the One who knows the beginning from the end, the One who is surprised by nothing, the One who can deliver you safely through the economic storms of our day.

THE FALL OF THE AMERICAN ECONOMY

Selected Scriptures

In this lesson we take an overview of America's deteriorating economic situation in light of biblical prophecy.

OUTLINE

In the past, the events which comprise historical shifts have happened over decades, if not centuries. But the decline in America's economic stability has happened so rapidly that we are witnesses to it worsening on a daily basis. The implications for the future are not positive.

    I. The Origin of the Ponzi Scheme

    II. The Ponzi Scheme of Social Security

    III. War and National Defense

    IV. The Growth of Big Government

    V. National and Private Debt

    VI. The Debt's Compounding Interest

    VII. The Cancer of Inflation

    VIII. The Specter of Bankruptcy

    IX. Today's Economic Meltdown in Biblical Prophecy

    X. Eroding Wealth

    XI. Erupting Wickedness

    XII. America's Puzzling Absence in Biblical Prophecy

    XIII. What Should We Do?

Most Americans are familiar with the scam perpetrated by Wall Street money manager Bernard Madoff, brought to light in 2008. Over two decades, Madoff cheated investment clients out of many billions of dollars—clients included many well-known celebrities, elderly retirees, and even his own sister. He used what is known as a Ponzi scheme, using the most recent infusion of funds from investors to show previous investors that their funds were earning a profit. Such schemes require what is ultimately their undoing: a continual stream of new investors and their money. While Madoff was feeding his clients falsified reports indicating their investments were making a profit, he was stealing their funds—until he got caught. In June 2009, Madoff was sentenced to 150 years in prison.

THE ORIGIN OF THE PONZI SCHEME

Ponzi schemes are named after Charles Ponzi who ran an investment scam in the early 1920s, promising investors outrageous returns which he paid with new investors' funds. He was sent to prison for a few years and then deported to his native Italy where he died in 1949.

Sadly, the American government is operating in a way not dissimilar to a Ponzi scheme, that is, living on borrowed money. We borrow money today to pay the interest on money we borrowed yesterday, going further and further in debt. It seems likely that, unless something changes, our national system of finance will collapse as surely as Ponzi schemes ultimately collapse. Living on borrowed money is unsustainable.

THE PONZI SCHEME OF SOCIAL SECURITY

Social Security began in 1935 under President Roosevelt to provide retirement assistance to those beyond working age. Survivor benefits were added in 1939 and Medicare benefits in 1965. By 2008, Social Security obligations had become one-third of the federal budget. Unfortunately, funds paid into Social Security by workers are not set aside for retirees like you would think. The government has been using Social Security revenue for years to pay for other government programs. As a result, Social Security is due to run out of funds— be unable to meet its obligations to retirees—in the near future.

When the huge Baby Boomer generation reaches full retirement in 2012, nearly 80 million Americans are going to be expecting their monthly Social Security check from the government, along with the Medicare benefits. But estimates are that the money will not be there to pay these obligations. The government has made promises it cannot keep.

WAR AND NATIONAL DEFENSE

You may be as shocked as I was to learn that, in 2008, 41.5 percent of all the military spending in the world belonged to the United States—more than China, Japan, Russia, Europe, and several other nations combined. In 2009, America's defense budget was $642 billion, second only to Social Security which was $677 billion. Those two items alone account for roughly two-thirds of America's budget.

Joel Belz, editor of *World* magazine, put these large numbers in a way that makes them memorable. He wrote in December 2009, "Wherever we stand on increasing our forces in Afghanistan, you'll have to concede that war is expensive. In round numbers, by some estimates, it cost a million dollars per soldier per year to send someone to Iraq or Afghanistan."[1] One million dollars, per soldier, per year. The war in Iraq was projected to cost less, around $50 billion; but so far it has cost almost $800 billion—and counting.

THE GROWTH OF BIG GOVERNMENT

The federal government began to balloon during the presidency of Franklin Roosevelt as a result of his "New Deal" programs designed to bring America out of the Great Depression. Then World War II resulted in an increase in the size of government. Additions of cabinet secretaries and their offices (education, commerce, transportation, and the rest) added enormous funding factors to the size of government. Today the federal government is HUGE, with annual employee salaries that dwarf those of workers in the private sector.

The United States government today is America's biggest employer. In 1900, only one of every twenty-four Americans worked for the government. By 1948 it was one in eight; and in 2009 there were nearly two million federal employees working for the government (one in five workers in America) with that number projected to rise by 15 percent in fiscal year 2010. The federal employees' payroll in 2009 was almost $15.5 billion.

The problem with 20 percent of American workers working for the government is that they produce no product—they are service employees. The government only spends money; it doesn't make money. (No, printing money doesn't count!) We're spending billions of dollars on government services that produce no income themselves.

NATIONAL AND PRIVATE DEBT

It cost the government $202 billion to service (pay the interest on) its debt (money it has borrowed from others) in 2009. Estimates are that, by 2019, it will cost $700 billion in interest payments alone on our $12 trillion in debt. Remember: interest payments don't reduce the debt; they just keep us from defaulting on the debt. We're doing nothing to pay down the actual principle of the debt.

If you factor in what the government's future entitlement (Social Security, Medicare) obligations are, the picture gets even more bleak. The current unfunded liability for Medicare part A (hospital care) is $36.7 trillion; for Part B (doctor visits) it's $37 trillion; for part D (prescription drugs) it's $15.6 trillion. The total liability of all three unfunded Medicare programs is $89.3 trillion. This is five times as much as the unfunded Social Security bill. So, if you add the unfunded liability of all three parts of Medicare to the unfunded liability of Social Security, you come up with a figure of $106.8 trillion dollars. Add to that last number our national debt of $14 trillion, and America's liabilities approach $120 trillion, or more than $380,000 per person in America (or $1.5 million for a family of four).

America's debts will not—cannot—be paid. We will simply keep rolling over the loans and paying interest on them like a person who pays only the interest on his credit card debt, or takes out a new credit card to pay off the debt on his current, "maxed out" card.

THE DEBT'S COMPOUNDING INTEREST

In 2009, America collected $904 billion in taxes from its citizens and paid out $383 billion in interest payments on our debt—or 42 percent of the federal revenue. And that did not touch the principle of our debts; it was all interest paid to our lenders (nations and individuals who have bought U.S. Treasury notes and bonds, which amount to loans from them to us). In 1952 we were indebted mainly to ourselves—to American citizens who had purchased U.S. savings bonds, Treasury notes, and other instruments. At the end of 2009, more than half of our nation's public debt is owed to foreign governments and financial institutions.

We owe $798.9 billion dollars to China, $746 billion to Japan, $230 billion to the United Kingdom, $188 billion to oil-exporting countries, $169 billion to the Caribbean banking centers, $156 billion to Brazil, $142 billion to Hong Kong, and, for the first time, we now owe $122.5 billion dollars to Russia. We did not owe Russia anything in 2007. Now, she is the eighth largest foreign holder of our debt.

Here are some "fun" facts about our debt: The interest grows at the rate of $41 million per hour; a one percent rise in the interest rate on our debt results in $80 billion more in interest owed; household debt—the debt of individual citizens—was $14 trillion in 2008.

THE CANCER OF INFLATION

As America's debt grows and her credit worthiness falls (the ability to repay her existing loans), we will be forced to raise the interest rates we offer to attract new lenders. Following those increased rates, the interest rates on money Americans borrow for homes, cars, and other items will also increase, making those items much more expensive. Existing dollars are also devalued when more paper dollars are printed by the government and put into the system—like the hundreds of billions of new dollars printed to stimulate the economy in 2008-2009—the infamous "bailout" money. The more money the Federal Reserve prints and injects into the system, the less each existing dollar is worth. It then takes more dollars to purchase the item "today" than it did "yesterday." And that's called inflation. Our government's leaders have created hundreds of billions of new dollars in the last two years to shore up failing financial institutions in an attempt to forestall a massive crisis that would throw the country into economic chaos. But they have only postponed the inevitable. At some point the bills will come due.

THE SPECTER OF BANKRUPTCY

When an individual can no longer pay his debts, he declares bankruptcy and walks away from his lenders. The same happens with a nation—it simply says, "Our debts are beyond our ability to pay, so we no longer acknowledge our debts." Leaders restructure the currency with an arbitrary value and life starts over. And revolution often follows. I think there is a good possibility that scenario is in America's future.

Citizens are recognizing that life in America has become scary. Rising unemployment, the government buying out car makers and banks to keep them from failing, other banks and businesses going bankrupt, mounting debts and deficits, devalued dollars, wars we cannot afford, Wall Street executives earning billions in bonuses— it's like nothing is "normal" anymore.

We have to turn to Scripture for counsel—how to respond to these critical times.

TODAY'S ECONOMIC MELTDOWN IN BIBLICAL PROPHECY

James 5:1-6 addresses a group of wealthy non-Christians who were amassing wealth in spite of the imminent return of Christ—they were oblivious to the age in which they were living. While there is nothing unbiblical about possessing wealth, their selfish use of their wealth made them ripe for judgment. God is interested in *how* we obtain wealth and *how* we use it. The wealthy non-Christians James addressed failed on both accounts. And there are many in our culture today failing on both accounts as well. They feel no accountability for their actions and are setting themselves up for judgment. America's riches have resulted in her becoming a byword among the nations.

ERODING WEALTH

James points out that the wealthy in his day were storing up corruptible wealth—wealth that would erode in value. America's wealth has greatly eroded. Our nation is bankrupt, unable to pay her debts. The dollar, which we have valued for so long, is losing its value.

Trillions of dollars of wealth have evaporated as home values have plummeted in the last two years and as the stock market has declined. Trillions of dollars—gone! Many of the nation's premier banking institutions had to be absorbed by other companies or propped up by government infusions of cash. The world's wealthiest people lost billions of dollars from their net worth. The number of billionaires in the world dropped from 1,100 to 700 between 2008 and 2009. The first decade of the twenty-first century will go down as the most economically chaotic since the Great Depression, a time when untold amounts of wealth vanished.

In Matthew 6:10-21, Jesus warned against storing up treasures on earth, advising His audience to store up treasures in heaven instead.

Erupting Wickedness

James criticized the unrighteous wealthy of his day for accumulating wealth in unjust ways: withholding pay from their employees. They were getting rich at the expense of others. This was a theme of the Old Testament prophets as well: "Woe to him who builds his house by unrighteousness and his chambers by injustice, who uses his neighbor's service without wages and gives him nothing for his work" (Jeremiah 22:13).

There is plenty of this going on today as well: lenders making loans to unqualified candidates; bankers promoting financial instruments they knew were doomed to fail; executives paying themselves huge bonuses on the strength of bailouts from the government; financial advisors like Bernard Madoff bilking clients out of their life savings. It's like the financial system has lost its moral compass. Bernie Madoff and others like him qualify well for the judgment spoken by James against the wicked wealthy of his day. People like this are interested only in their own personal gain regardless of what happens to others. They are forerunners of a one-world ruler destined to capture the entire world's wealth for his own selfish ends.

America's Puzzling Absence in Biblical Prophecy

In my book, *What in the World Is Going On?* I devoted a chapter to the question of America in biblical prophecy. Does America have a role in biblical prophecy according to Scripture? The short answer is "No"—but there is more to be said on the subject. Some students of prophecy think America will be absorbed into the revived Roman Empire, the European Union. Others believe America may be invaded, while others think America's moral decay will lead to its demise before Christ returns.

I once held to the view that the Rapture would remove so many people from America (perhaps one-fourth of the population) that America would be terminally weakened and disrupted. But what if America's debt burden causes her to become the literal servant of her lenders? What if our once-great nation becomes so weakened because of its crippling debt burden that it is simply absorbed into the coming New World Order and loses its identity as the world's leading symbol of strength, freedom, and financial stability? I don't know if that is what will play out at the end of the age, but it could. And the further in debt America goes, the greater the possibility that something similar could happen.

WHAT SHOULD WE DO?

The writer to the Hebrews gave his readers excellent financial advice: "Let your conduct be without covetousness; be content with such things as you have. For He Himself has said, 'I will never leave you nor forsake you'" (Hebrews 13:5). In other words, Christians are not to desire more for the sake of having more. We are to live contented lives with our hope in the never-failing presence of Christ, our Lord, to be our security. We should continually derive our values about work, money, ethics, and morality from Scripture rather than from the world. Difficult financial times shouldn't tempt us to live a disobedient life; we should be as faithful in days of difficulty as we are in days of ease.

The Bible says that life on planet earth will become very dark and difficult prior to the return of Christ, so we should not be surprised at what we see happening in our world. These days should motivate us to take the Gospel and our understanding of biblical prophecy to a world living in confusion and despair. We have the only message that will survive the present and future upheavals the world may witness. May God grant us the courage to speak and live with biblical clarity in the days ahead.

Note:

1. Joel Belz, "Up, Up and Up. On Almost Every Front, It's Been an Inflationary Year," *World*, December 19, 2009, 6.

APPLICATION

1. Read Deuteronomy 15:4b-6.

   a. What economic condition did God promise to the Israelites? (verse 4b)

   b. What was the condition for such a promise being fulfilled? (verse 5)

   c. How was that promise to be manifested in Israel's relations with other nations? (verse 6)

   d. How would you evaluate America's lender/borrower status in light of that promise to Israel?

   e. What connection is there between verses 5 and 6 in the case of America? (America is not Israel, so how should we interpret promises like this? What principle is there to follow?)

f. Why would 2 Chronicles 7:14 be a good place for America to start when it comes to reversing her economic peril?

g. How would you reconcile verse 4 with verse 11 (see also Matthew 26:11)? (Hint: Is obedience to verse 5 the bridge between the two possibilities of "no poor" and "poor" among you?)

2. How would you apply the "a" and "b" parts of Psalm 33:12 to America? What lesson is there in this verse for America?

3. What does Proverbs 22:7 say about borrowers and lenders?

a. Which label applies to America today—borrower or lender?

b. That means America is now a _____ to other nations of the world. (See Proverbs 22:7)

c. Why do borrowers ultimately become the servant of lenders?

d. In your own financial life, to whom have you become a servant?

e. Compare Proverbs 22:7 with Paul's admonition in Romans 13:8. Why did Paul want Christians to live debt free.

f. How would America be different if she heeded the admonition of Romans 13:8?

g. Can what happens to poor individuals also happen to poor nations—to America? What evidence do you see for this already happening? (Proverbs 14:20; 19:4)

h. What might America end up doing one day if her debt situation is not reversed? (Proverbs 18:23)

4. What lessons from America's situation can you draw and apply to your own financial life?

DID YOU KNOW?

When we read about "billions" and "trillions" in the news, it's hard to picture those amounts. This may help: The Federal Reserve issues new hundred-dollar bills to banks in small packs of 100 bills each, or $10,000 per pack. One hundred of those packs equals $1,000,000. Ten thousand of those packs equals $100,000,000—the amount that can sit on a standard industrial pallet in a neat cube of bills. Ten of those pallets could fit in the average living room, holding $1,000,000,000. Ten thousand of those pallets, enough to fill a fair-sized warehouse, would hold $1,000,000,000,000, or one trillion dollars. You could spend a million dollars a day, every day since the birth of Christ, and still not spend a trillion dollars.

THE NEW WORLD ORDER

Selected Scriptures

In this lesson we examine why Christians should oppose the current trend toward a one world government.

OUTLINE

Chaos and crisis are breeding grounds for revolution, the rise of despotic leaders, and totalitarian governments. Such changes have taken place within nations many times in history, but never at an international level. Current calls for a new world order violate God's plan for nation-states.

I. **The Ancient Appearance of a New World Order**

II. **The Modern Attempt at a New World Order**

III. **The Future Arrival of a New World Order**

IV. **What's Wrong With Pursuing a New World Order?**
   A. It Promises a Peace It Cannot Produce
   B. It Presumes a Unity That Is Impossible
   C. It Paves the Way for a One World Ruler
   D. It Produces the Roadmap for a Global Economy

There is a shrinking percentage of the population that was old enough in 1938 to remember a scary Halloween radio broadcast—the CBS *Mercury Theatre on the Air*—that adapted a scenario from H. G. Wells' novel, *The War of the Worlds*. It was the first time a fictional broadcast had been presented in the format of a news bulletin, so almost everyone who heard it took it seriously. The broadcast said the United States was under invasion by people from the planet Mars! All across America, hysteria reigned. Communication then wasn't like today—it took days to get the word out via radio and newspapers that the whole broadcast was a hoax, and it took even longer to convince people that there was no invasion.

The War of the Worlds was not H. G. Wells' only scary book. Another book he wrote, *The New World Order*, predicted a "United States of the World" a world in which nations came to solve their international problems together in the pursuit of world peace.

In 1977, the space vehicles Voyager I and II carried a message into space to enlighten anyone who might find it that the United States of America was a nation in a world moving toward a "single global civilization." We have President Jimmy Carter to thank for that initiative, and president George H. W. Bush to thank for another on September 11, 1990—his references to a "new world order" in a speech to Congress. Four months later, in another speech, President Bush talked again about a "new world order." And in November 2008, Henry Kissinger used the same phrase—"new world order"—to talk about the direction in which the world is rapidly moving. The implication of his remarks was that the new President Obama is the one who can bring about this new alignment of nations.

But it's not just politicians, presidents, and statesmen who are in favor of such a world-changing union. Pope Benedict XVI, in a June 2009 encyclical letter, called for "a true world political authority . . . with the effective power to ensure security for all."[1] Iranian president Ahmadinejad has made similar statements.

As "positive" as these pronouncements seem, economist Larry Bates interprets them differently:

"I have said for many years that the term new world order is merely a code word for one world socialism with an elite ruling class to govern the rest of us under their demonic system."[2]

In this lesson, we will look at what the Bible says about the possibility of a "new world order" at the end of the age—and why it is not a positive development and is not from God.

THE ANCIENT APPEARANCE OF A NEW WORLD ORDER

The first "new world order" is described in Genesis 11—the gathering that took place in Shinar where the idea for the Tower of Babel was birthed. This was after Noah's Flood, when the entire human race spoke the same language and lived in what is now modern Iraq. The people decided to build a great tower in search of security (it was a symbol of strength) and significance ("Look at us!"). Instead of depending on God for strength and security, they sought to find it in themselves.

Paul says in Acts 17:26-27 that God appointed the boundaries of nations "so that they should seek the Lord." But instead of seeking the Lord, the inhabitants of Shinar decided to reach to the heavens with a great tower—much as Satan did before being cast out of heaven by God: "I will ascend into heaven . . . I will exalt my throne above the stars . . . I will be like the Most High" (Isaiah 14:13-14).

The first world order set themselves in opposition to God as their ruler. Instead of spreading out and inhabiting and populating the earth as God had commanded (Genesis 9:7), they drew together and became a government of the new, post-Flood world. God looked at the potential for human rebellion in their actions and decided to put a stop to it. So He confused their language, forcing them to decentralize into smaller language groups and to spread out.

"Internationalism"—a one world government—was not God's plan in the beginning, nor is it now. God's plan is "nationalism"—a family of nations spread across the earth (Acts 17:26-27). Only when Christ rules the earth from His throne in Jerusalem during the coming Millennium will there be a God-ordained "new world order" (Revelation 20:1-10).

THE MODERN ATTEMPT AT A NEW WORLD ORDER

The United Nations is the most well-known, modern attempt at establishing a new world order—and the United States is the largest contributor to its funding. The 18 acres on which the U.N. sits in New York City is international territory—the property of the world, not of New York City or America.

The U.N. buildings are filled with biblical references and images of peace, donated by member nations. The most well-known is the Russian sculpture of a man beating a sword into a plowshare, based on Isaiah 2:4 and Micah 4:3. An enormous stained-glass window by Jewish artist Marc Chagall features the Tree of Life from the Garden of Eden, the serpent, and the cross of Christ.

In spite of all this biblical imagery and good intentions, the United Nations has been a bureaucracy that has not accomplished its goal of creating peace between the nations of the world. In fact, some of its actions seem ludicrous, such as creating a Human Rights Commission in 2006 with nations like Sudan, Zimbabwe, China, Russia, and Saudi Arabia as members— some of the biggest human rights abusing nations in the world!

United Nations peacekeepers have failed to prevent genocide in places like Bosnia and Darfur. Palestine has received far more recognition and support than has Israel and the Jewish people. And ruthless dictators like Hugo Chavez (Venezuela), Mahmoud Ahmadinejad (Iran), and Muammar Gaddafi (Libya) are given the podium, free to attack anything and everything without limits.

The U.N. has been a failed attempt to unite the world under a banner of unity and peace.

THE FUTURE ARRIVAL OF A NEW WORLD ORDER

In spite of past and present failures of new world orders, one is coming in the future that is a good and godly one: the Millennium, during which Jesus Christ will rule the world for a thousand years. It will be instituted following the seven-year Tribulation, which follows the Rapture of the Church of Jesus Christ—the removal of true believers from the earth so they avoid the terrible judgments of the Tribulation period.

The Old Testament prophets saw the coming reign of the Messiah as a time of peace, extending even to the animal kingdom (Isaiah 11:6-9). In short, the creation-peace that was prevalent naturally in the Garden of Eden—complete harmony between man, animals, and God—will be restored by fiat by Christ. War and rebellion will end (Isaiah 2:4) as a result of Satan being bound for the thousand-year period (Revelation 20:1-3). Psalm 72 also indicates that the Millennium will be a time of justice and prosperity. King David will be resurrected and be a co-regent with Jesus Christ over all the earth (Jeremiah 30:9; Ezekiel 34:23-24; Hosea 3:5).

In a world filled with sin, peace is impossible. We are admonished to live in peace with all men (Romans 12:18); but that is an individual instruction, not a national one. Strength is the only virtue that can bring about peace at a "world" level. Only strength can deter aggression. And if strength is bargained away at the table of political correctness or appeasement of our enemies, there will be no peace.

WHAT'S WRONG WITH PURSUING A NEW WORLD ORDER?

There are four reasons why attempting to set up a new world order is a bad idea.

It Promises Peace It Cannot Produce

No one can promise peace and deliver peace except God. Thus any new world order that is not of God will fail. There are wars being fought in our world at this very moment—man has been incapable of bringing about world peace and unity. Peace treaties are written and broken regularly.

The Bible says a world dictator is coming in the future who will promise peace and actually deliver it for a very short time. People will be so hungry for peace that they will pledge their allegiance to this new leader. He will be rising on the international stage when Christ returns for His church at the Rapture. Signs of peace will appear. Peace will unfold during the first half of the seven-year Tribulation as the world leader brokers a peace treaty between Israel and the nations aligned against her. The nations are lulled into submissiveness by his success at bringing about peace. He uses his success as leverage to continue forming his new world order. But Daniel 8:25 foretells that "by peace [he] shall destroy many."

The Antichrist's peace will last for only three-and-one-half years. He himself breaks the peace treaty he established with Israel and turns on the nation. It is only another example of sinful man's failed attempts to bring about anything righteous and pure.

It Presumes a Unity That Is Impossible

Back in 1971, the famous member of the Beatles, John Lennon, wrote a song called "Imagine." It was an international hit during a very chaotic time in American culture. The lyrics appealed to young people's longing for peace and purpose in life. Lennon called on his listeners to imagine a world in which there was no heaven, no hell, no countries, nothing to kill or die for, no religion, no possessions, and no need for greed or hunger. He called on people to imagine living for today and living life in peace. The result, he sang, would be a world that lived as one.

It is a beautiful song and describes a beautiful world—and it captured the attention and emotions of an entire generation with its utopian vision. Unfortunately it suggested no mechanism, no way to bring about the world it described. It ignored the same thing that every utopian dream has ignored: the sinfulness of man. Jeremiah 17:9 says, "The heart is deceitful above all things, and desperately wicked; who can know it?" Nothing that man does escapes the taint of sin, and that includes his efforts to create a one world government, a new world order. It was the British author and apologist C. S. Lewis who said, "No clever arrangement of rotten eggs will make a good omelet." That is also true when it comes to the best-laid plans of man. They originate in a sinful heart and therefore have no hope of establishing a righteous result.

It Paves the Way for a One World Ruler

Besides promising a peace it can't deliver and presuming unity is possible, a new world order is also an engraved invitation for a one world ruler to ascend to power. This is not a new possibility, it is a historical reality. The economic desperation in Germany prior to World War II set the stage for Adolf Hitler to become the despotic dictator of that nation. People get desperate and are willing to believe the promises of anyone who seems to be capable of delivering them from desperate times. And it's happened at other times in history as well. Economic and world chaos is a birthing ground for a ruler who makes promises he can't keep. And people end up in a worse situation than before.

The nations of the world are looking for someone who can provide direction and solutions to the problems of economics, war, hunger, climate change, and other crises both regional and international. People want peace and affluence; they want problems to go away. And they are willing to give up a measure of freedom to anyone who can keep the enemy at bay and keep money in their pockets. The character of the leader, or the means he uses to accomplish his goals, is not as important as whether he can deliver on his promises.

Daniel 7 and Revelation 13 tell us that such a leader will arise on the world stage one day. He will be a leader of great charisma and persuasive powers of speech. He will be attractive, a powerful orator, and a messiah-like figure who will be worshiped by the world. With cultic capability, he will take charge of a desperate world and bring order out of chaos. He will use the world's economic systems to fund and fuel his selfish ambitions. He will be the opposite of the godly leader the world needs and thus will be known as the Antichrist.

It Produces the Roadmap for a Global Economy

There will be an attempt in the future to violate the principle of Acts 17—the principle of nation-states into which God has divided the world—and create an international state with a global economy. We are seeing a miniature, failed version of such a plan today in Europe. As of this writing, many economists and analysts are predicting the demise of the Euro, the paper currency created out of nothing and with no inherent value (like the U.S. dollar) to serve the European Union. The need to rescue the economy of Greece added impetus to the decline of the value of the Euro on world markets. And if Greece's fate also becomes the fate of other indebted nations like Italy, Portugal, and Spain, the Euro could collapse altogether. So this attempt at a regional economy does not bode well for the success of a global economy in the future.

As Christians today, we must be very discerning about all that is happening in our nation and in our world. It's easy to be swept up in policies and programs ostensibly designed to be for our nation's benefit, only to find out that they have led us down a slippery path. As a nation, we are living where God planned for us to live—in a nation called America (Acts 17:26). There is only one time appointed for a one world government, and that is when Jesus Christ returns to rule for the thousand-year Millennium. Until then, we must be careful about being pulled into international alliances that are not consistent with God's plan for nation-states.

We are not to be globalists or internationalists. We are not to be isolationists either—America has done more good in the world in terms of aid and charity to others than any nation in history. So we must remain engaged with our near and far neighbors. But in doing so, we must not fall prey to the present and future calls for a new world order and one world government.

Let us ask God for wisdom in dealing with pressures that will surely come in the days ahead as we wait for Christ, the King of Kings, to gather us to Himself. In Him alone will we find true peace and justice.

Notes:

1. Benedict XVI, Caritas in Veritate, Encyclical Letter, 29 June 2009, http://www.vatican.va/holy_father/benedict_xvi/encyclicals/documents/ hf_ben-xvi_enc_20090629_caritas-in-veritate_en.html#_edn146

2. Larry Bates, *The New Economic Disorder*, (Lake Mary, FL: Excel Books, 2009), 22.

APPLICATION

1. Read Acts 17:24-31.

   a. What initial assumptions about God does Paul make when speaking to the Greek scholars in Athens? (verse 24)

   b. Scan through Paul's speech (verses 22-31) and look for references to Christ. Why did Paul begin and end this message to the Greeks the way He did?

   c. Why did Paul make reference to "temples made with hands"? (verse 24) See if you can find information about the "Areopagus" for a clue. (verse 22)

   d. What does "one blood" refer to in verse 26?

   e. What has God ordained concerning the peoples of the earth? (verse 26)

f. How is Psalm 139:16 a personal version of the national design found in verse 26?

g. How do these verses impact your thinking about your own national heritage and identity?

h. Does Paul's point in verse 26 support the idea of God having a purpose for America? What do you think are some purposes God may have designed for America to fulfill?

i. How has America changed since its founding? Are we still accomplishing the purposes the founding fathers decreed for this nation?

j. What reason did Paul give for God dividing the world into nations with boundaries? (verse 27)

k. What ought all nations realize in spite of their differences? (verse 28)

l. What has God overlooked (been patient with) in the history of the nations of the world? (verses 29-30)

m. What message is now being sent to the nations of the world concerning Christ and His Gospel? (verse 30)

n. Why is God giving the opportunity for the nations to repent? (verse 31)

o. What sign did God give that Christ is to be the judge of the nations? (verse 31)

2. What warning does Paul give to Christians in 2 Thessalonians 2:3 concerning the future of the world? Would Paul give such a warning if it were not possible for Christians to be deceived?

DID YOU KNOW?

The closest thing to an international pan-national government today is the European Union which consists of 27 member nations—from Scandinavian nations in the north to Mediterranean border nations in the south of Europe. The European Union has grown from an initial treaty in 1952 to the most recent Lisbon Treaty in December 2009. The EU encompasses a half-billion people and an estimated Gross Domestic Product of $14.8 trillion. It has its own currency (the Euro) in addition to the currencies of 11 member nations. The EU has its own government, courts, laws, and policy-making bodies, and participates in international meetings such as the G-8, G-20, WTO, and the United Nations.

THE NEW GLOBAL ECONOMY

Selected Scriptures

*In this lesson we examine the ever-increasing presence
of the "global economy."*

OUTLINE

Just a few decades ago, making a purchase from another country or
traveling to a foreign country was complicated and expensive. Today,
it is seamless. The electronic financial net surrounding the earth has
created a global economy, setting the stage for end-time realities.

I.   **The Birth of the Global Economy**

II. **Preparing for the End Times Economy**
  A. Influential Global Institutions
  B. A Global Regulatory Board
  C. The Growing Influence of Europe
  D. Instantaneous Global Money Transfer

III. **New Attitudes for a New World**
  A. Mendacity (Deception)
  B. Stupidity
  C. Arrogance
  D. Greed

In 1929, the global depression hit Germany and gave Adolf Hitler the opportunity to make his move to gain control. German banks closed, inflation was rampant, unemployment was widespread, and into the chaos stepped the modern era's most diabolical leader. And the people welcomed him as a savior. Tyrants take advantage of crises. They even engineer them: They create the problem and then offer themselves as the solution.

A series of crises in the United States has led to our government gaining more and more control in our society. Government mortgage policies resulted in a sub-prime mortgage crisis, so the government stepped in to bail out banks deemed "too big to fail." Government became an owner in two car companies (General Motors and Chrysler) and the two largest mortgage-backing companies ("Fannie Mae" and "Freddie Mac"). And they provided billions of dollars in loans to banks—all done with money the government borrowed and printed. Then the government took over one-sixth of the United States economy by legislating mandatory, government-run health care—requiring citizens to participate under penalty of law.

Given what we have witnessed in America in the last two years, it is not difficult to see how a one world government could gradually assume more and more control over the entire world economy.

THE BIRTH OF THE GLOBAL ECONOMY

Most economists and historians mark 1944 as the beginning of the global economy. Seven-hundred-thirty leading representatives from 44 allied nations gathered in Bretton Woods, New Hampshire, in an historic hotel to lay plans for reconstructing the world's economy following World War II. Rules for monetary policy, global commerce, international trade, and currency exchange rates were discussed. Three new movements resulted from the Bretton Woods meeting: The International Monetary Fund (IMF), the World Bank Group, and the General Agreement on Tariffs and Trade. Each participating country at Bretton Woods committed itself to a monetary policy based on the gold standard; gold was pegged at $35 per ounce. In retrospect, analysts today believe that the delegates to the conference intended for the Bretton Woods meeting to lay a foundation for a one world economic system as a partial means to preventing further international conflicts like World War II.

The U.S. dollar was established as the "reserve currency" of the world because America had the largest and most stable economy of any nation. We also had more units of currency circulating than any other national currency. Even though America disconnected its currency from the gold standard in 1971, the U.S. dollar has remained the world's reserve currency— meaning other countries of the world value their currencies against the U.S. dollar. Also, commodities like gold and oil are priced in terms of U.S. dollars. When other nations of the world buy these commodities, they pay an exchange rate to convert their currency to dollars in order to purchase the commodities. America saves on those exchange rates since our currency is already the dollar.

But things are changing—the U.S. dollar is losing its grip on the reserve currency status. America's reputation for stability—the main reason the dollar has been the world's go-to currency—is slipping. Our mounting debt is causing other nations to be less secure about the long-term value and stability of holding dollars in reserve. This is a major shift in America's history and in the world economy. It creates a vacuum of confidence into which another currency or leader or economic system could step.

America has become illiquid—our debts are greater than our income. We are kept alive only by borrowing money from other nations. (Most Americans are unaware of this fact, I fear.) Yet we continue to spend money and give money to other, poorer nations. But this can go on for only so long before the house of debt comes crashing down.

The major nations of the world recognize America's problem and have been quietly buying up gold instead of U.S. dollars. This means they have more confidence in gold than in America's currency —for the first time in modern history. And individual investors, including Americans, are beginning to buy gold as well—gold coins and bullion. The reason? They fear the U.S. dollar might be worthless one day—and gold has never, in 5,000 years, been worthless. It has been the standard for wealth in all of recorded history.

At the April 2009, G-8 Summit, the president of Russia called on the nations of the world to create a new reserve currency that would transcend national boundaries and authorities—a currency to replace the U.S. dollar. The other BRIC nations (Brazil, Russia, India, China) joined Russia in calling for a new international reserve currency later that year. There has been a growing swell of support for this movement from other leaders as well.

Why should America have to take this development seriously? Because "the borrower is servant to the lender" (Proverbs 22:7)! We are in debt to all the major nations of the world. We are in no place to argue with them. If they stop loaning us money America would collapse into chaos. Most Americans are not aware of how serious our nation's predicament is.

The British economist, John Maynard Keynes, considered by many to be the architect of modern (debt-based) economic theory, quoted Vladimir Lenin in one of his books—words that have frightening implications for today. Lenin said,

> By continuing the process of inflation, governments can confiscate, secretly and unobserved, an important part of the wealth of their citizens...There is no subtler, no surer means of overturning the existing basis of society than to debauch the currency. The process engages all the hidden forces of economic law on the side of destruction, and it does so in a manner that not one man in a million is able to diagnose.[1]

Whether on purpose or not, that is what is happening in America. Our currency is being rapidly devalued by the government's printing of new money and injecting it into the economy. The percentage of dollars individuals hold becomes a smaller and smaller "piece of the pie" with the majority of the money under the control of the government, in our case, the Federal Reserve. Some of you are old enough to remember when something that you now pay several dollars for cost a dollar or less—evidence of the devaluing of our currency.

There are changes taking place in America—changes that will likely never be reversed. We are entering unprecedented ground as a nation. Our loss of influence may make it easier in the future for the nations of the world to unite in a new world economic order, with or without our approval.

PREPARING FOR THE END TIMES ECONOMY

Looking at biblical prophecy, we will find that the economic instability in the world, leading to a new global economy, was foreseen ages ago.

Influential Global Institutions

Two institutions already exist that could provide a framework for a new global economy: the World Bank and the IMF (International Monetary Fund) both created in 1944. These institutions are part of the economic life of almost every nation on earth in one way or another. The infrastructure is in place that would allow new priorities and agendas to be rolled out. We have become so accustomed to their presence in the world economy that it would not come as a shock if they began slowly increasing their presence and role at an international level. Most people in America may have heard of these institutions, but few could define their purpose and role. Therefore, if they began doing something different, few people would take notice.

A Global Regulatory Board

At the April 2009 meeting of the G-20 nations—the 20 most powerful economic nations in the world—the discussion was all about the global financial crisis that began in 2008. These 19 nations, plus the European Union (counted as one of the G-20 members), represent 90 percent of the world's gross national product, 80 percent of world trade, and two-thirds of the world's population.[2]

A Financial Stability Board was put in place representing all the member countries, made up of financial, banking, trade, and economic experts from each country. In short, the purpose of this Board is to oversee and regulate the global economy. They will supposedly monitor financial activities in the world economy in order to identify risks that could lead to the kind of financial meltdown that began in 2008. Since the Board is new, it remains to be seen what kind of authority they exercise, and whether member nations will submit the governance of their country's economy to the recommendation of the Board. But, in principle, this could very easily happen since the purpose of the Board is to say, "Do this or that" to the member countries.

This is new! Nothing like this has ever existed in the world before. It is another example of nations sacrificing a bit more of their sovereignty to a world-level organization. Fewer and fewer people will be making decisions that affect more and more individuals.

From a prophetic perspective, organizations like the World Bank, the IMF, and the new Financial Stability Board will make it easy for the coming Antichrist to control the world's economy (Revelation 13:16; 14:9).

The Growing Influence of Europe

Europe's growing influence is also predicted in biblical prophecy since it represents the revival of the fourth beast—the Roman Empire—in Daniel's prophetic visions. Three of the kingdoms have come and vanished: Babylon, Medo-Persia, and Greece. The fourth, Rome, was never completely destroyed; it gradually faded away. That leaves its final destruction to take place in the future, requiring its resurrection beforehand. Today's Europe represents the ancient Roman Empire. In Daniel's prophecy, it is Christ who destroys the fourth empire which can only happen at His Second Coming.

I believe the European nations represent a revived form of the ancient Roman Empire, the fourth kingdom in Daniel's visions. Europe is more organized and integrated than at any time in history since the days of Rome and is already considered to be the second most powerful economic force in the world. It was European leaders who called for the global summit to deal with the economic crisis. Thirty-six of the 50 largest financial corporations in the world are headquartered in Europe. And the Bible predicts that the anti-Christ will come from the revived fourth empire. Besides Israel, Europe is the most prophecy-relevant region of the world to watch.

Instantaneous Global Money Transfer

"Electronic" commerce is fast becoming the norm in the world today. Consumers, governments, companies—everyone can buy and sell internationally, thanks to the Internet and global commerce. For example, credit card companies like MasterCard are developing the means to transfer money from one MasterCard to another MasterCard or MaestroCard anywhere in the world. The goal is to lower the barriers to international commerce, to make buying and selling on the other side of the world as easy as at your corner grocery store. The credit card companies make all the appropriate currency exchange calculations instantaneously based on current exchange rates. The net effect? It's like having a global currency. It will gradually prepare people to think in terms of hundreds of currencies becoming one currency, since all currency conversions happen behind the scenes.

New Attitudes for a New World

A cartoon by Edward Sorel, titled "The Four Horsemen of the Wall Street Apocalypse," is a play on the four horsemen of Revelation 6—the traditional "Four Horsemen of the Apocalypse."[3] Sorel labeled his four horsemen mendacity (deception), stupidity, arrogance, and greed—his way of characterizing modern national and international finance. Those four traits are certainly spoken against in Scripture; and in order to understand what's happening and will happen in international finance, we have to understand the nature of the human heart.

Mendacity (Deception)

The world is full of financial deception and fraud. The prophet Ezekiel spoke strongly against taking bribes to increase one's financial gain: "'In you they take bribes to shed blood; you take usury and increase; you have made profit from your neighbors by extortion, and have forgotten Me says the Lord God'" (Ezekiel 22:12-13).

From Internet scams to sophisticated Wall Street Ponzi schemes, deception is rampant. The largest investment bank on Wall Street was just called to account by Congress for selling financial products to their customers that they themselves were dumping from their institutional accounts. We think such actions are dishonest and unconscionable, but they are standard practice in today's world. The sub-prime mortgage crisis was caused by lenders approving mortgages for applicants they knew could never make the payments. Deception may bring down the entire financial system someday.

Stupidity

I'm using the cartoonist's words here—"stupid" is a harsh (though not unbiblical— Proverbs 12:1; 30:2) word, yet it seems to apply. People do some pretty foolish things today in their pursuit of wealth—they fall prey to get-rich-quick schemes, and lose their money. The apostle Paul wrote to Timothy that "the love of money is the root of all kinds of evil" (1 Timothy 6:9-10), and that greed has caused some to stray from the faith.

Wealth isn't the problem; greed is the problem. Money isn't the problem; love of money is the problem. When people act stupidly with money, it is usually because they are pursuing some illegal, unreasonable, or irresponsible means of getting more.

Arrogance

Paul also tells Timothy to "command those who are rich in this present age not to be haughty" (1 Timothy 6:17). That certainly applies to most people who live in America and who will be reading this study guide—we are "rich in this present age" compared to most of the world's people.

God has blessed us richly by letting us live in a country where it is possible to earn more than enough to live on. But we should never let our abundance become the source of our life; we have no right to take pride in something that is the result of God's blessing. Pride and arrogance come before a fall, Scripture says, and God opposes the proud (Proverbs 16:18; James 4:6).

Greed

Greed is no doubt the trait most associated with the current financial collapse. Greed ranged from people buying homes they couldn't afford to Wall Street executives doing whatever deal would result in the largest year-end bonus. C. S. Lewis wrote that unhealthy and inordinate desires create an "ever-increasing craving for an ever-diminishing pleasure"[4]—the best definition of greed I've ever read.

When people become dissatisfied with their possessions or standard of living, it's easy to compromise values and standards "just this once." But then dissatisfaction sets in again, and compromise, driven by greed, becomes easier. No wonder the apostle Paul, after warning Timothy about the love of money, told him to "flee these things and pursue righteousness, godliness, faith, love, patience, gentleness" (1 Timothy 6:11).

It is time for Christ's true believers to pursue these traits instead of mendacity, stupidity, arrogance, and greed—traits that will grow more prevalent as the global economy expands.

Notes:

1. John Maynard Keynes, *The Economic Consequences of the Peace* (New York: Harcourt, Brace, and Howe, 1920), 148-149.

2. Group of 20 Updated September 25, 2009, *The New York Times,* http://topics.nytimes.com/top/reference/timestopics/organizations/g/group_of_20/index.html, (accessed 16 February 2010).

3. Joseph Stiglitz, "Wall Street's Toxic Message," *Vanity Fair,* July 2009, <http://www.vanityfair.com/politics/features/2009/07/third-world-debt200907> (accessed 5 October 2009).

4. C. S. Lewis, *Screwtape Letters* in *The Complete C. S. Lewis Signature Classics* (New York: HarperCollins Publishers, Inc., 2002), 143.

1. Read Daniel 7:23-27.

   a. What is Daniel explaining in this part of his interpretation of his dream? (verse 23)

   b. How is the fourth kingdom characterized? (verse 23)

   c. What do the horns represent? (verse 24) How is the single horn that arises characterized? (verse 25)

   d. What happens to his power? (verses 25-27)

   e. Whose kingdom will ultimately replace this king's kingdom? (verse 27)

   f. Since God's kingdom has not yet been established on earth, when might we expect this king to arise?

2. Describe the kinds of things that were happening financially in Israel which displeased the Lord? (Ezekiel 22:12-13)

   a. What was God's response? What would His judgment entail? (verses 14-16)

   b. How does Jesus' response in Mark 11:15 parallel God's response to financial impropriety in Israel?

   c. How do Jesus' words in Luke 12:15 provide a paradigm for viewing the place "money" should have in one's life?

   d. Of what does your life consist? What role does money play?

3. Read 1 Timothy 6:6-19.

   a. What does Paul say is our greatest source of gain in life? (verse 6)

b. What principle should govern our "attachment" to material wealth? (verse 7)

c. How would you apply verse 8 to the modern era? Is it wrong to possess more than "food and clothing"? (verse 8)

d. What is the danger that accompanies a "love of money" (verses 9-10)

e. How have you seen this principle illustrated in your life, or the life of someone you know?

f. What kinds of "sorrows" (verse 10) often accompany the love of money?

g. What should the Christian be pursuing instead of the accumulation of wealth? (verses 11-12)

h. What advice does Paul give to the rich? (verse 17) How does this advice compare with Jesus' words to the young man in Luke 18:22? Why the different advice?

i. How do you personally balance your enjoyment (verse 17) of possessions with the temptation to value them as ends in themselves?

DID YOU KNOW?

"G-20" is a shorthand way of referring to the "Group of Twenty Finance Ministers and Central Bank Governors," a group of ministers of finance and central bank leaders from 19 countries of the world plus the European Union (a collection of 27 nations represented as one in the G-20). The 20 members of the G-20 are South Africa, Argentina, Brazil, Mexico, Canada, United States, China, Japan, South Korea, India, Indonesia, Saudi Arabia, France, Germany, Italy, Russia, Turkey, United Kingdom, Australia, plus the European Union. In addition to these countries'/union's leaders, the leaders of the International Monetary Fund and the World Bank also participate in G-20 meetings.

From Crisis to Consolidation

Selected Scriptures

In this lesson we learn how a short-term national crisis can lead to a long-term national calamity.

OUTLINE

Sometimes revolutions happen overnight—old governments are replaced by new. More often, change is gradual. Citizens cede their rights to the government in exchange for security and provision. That happened in Egypt in Joseph's day, and it could happen to us in our day.

I. **Causes and Evidences of Power Consolidation**
   A. The Federal Budget
   B. The Banking Institutions
   C. Financial Regulation
   D. The Stock Market

II. **The Famine Forecast**

III. **Joseph's Plan for a Centralized Government**

IV. **Joseph's Plan for Survival**
   A. The Consolidation of the Egyptians' Livelihood
   B. The Consolidation of the Egyptians' Livestock
   C. The Consolidation of the Egyptians' Land
   D. The Consolidation of the Egyptians' Location
   E. The Consolidation of the Egyptians' Labor

V. **Was Joseph a Hero or a Tyrant?**

VI. **The Long-Term Result of Power Consolidation**
   A. Sacrificing Tomorrow on the Altar of Today
   B. Submitting the Good of Many to the Control of One

In May 2010 the European Union and the International Monetary Fund agreed on a $140 billion bailout plan for Greece—a bankrupt nation. But the plan was met with mostly negative reactions around the world and especially in Greece. There were riots in that country, and the value of the Euro currency continued its downward spiral after a short rally on the news of the bailout.

Greece may be only the first in a chain of European nations that could default on their obligations. Known as the PIIGS, they include Portugal, Ireland, Italy, Greece, and Spain. England's prime minister was just defeated in a bid for reelection, in large part due to England's fiscal crisis. And we have already discussed America's illiquid condition with debt obligations that far outweigh her capacity to repay. America continues to struggle to make gains in employment and productivity. Food pantries are finding their cupboards bare as more and more people line up to receive free food.

We are living in an age when the potential for social revolution (seeds of which were sown recently in Greece) is extremely high in democratic countries. People are losing confidence in government to fix existing problems. They are realizing that big spending, debt-happy governments have become part of the problem rather than the solution. Absent of any better solutions, people grow more and more willing to lend their support to whoever can step in and make a difference. But this willingness to give up freedom for provision is a trend that will have dire consequences in the future. Power is being consolidated in high places, out of the reach of the average citizen.

CAUSES AND EVIDENCES OF POWER CONSOLIDATION

In his book, *When a Nation Forgets God*, Erwin Lutzer writes, "After the fall of the Berlin wall a cartoon appeared in a Russian newspaper picturing a fork in the road. One path was labeled *freedom*; the other path was labeled *sausage*. As we might guess, the path to freedom had few takers; the path to sausage was crowded with footprints. When given a choice, most people probably will choose bread and sausage above the free market and individual liberties. It was Lenin's promise of bread in every kitchen that ignited the communist revolution. Bread with political slavery was better than freedom and starvation. Bread fills the stomach, freedom does not."[1]

In times of despair, people often move to accept a strong centralized government to provide for them. America's founding fathers created a republic with decentralized state governments rather than one, all-controlling federal government. Sadly, our nation is shifting more and more in the direction of centralized power as indicated by the following.

The Federal Budget

The size and influence of the federal government has increased dramatically in recent years and, given the programs to which it has committed itself in only the last two years, the size will continue to grow. We are heading toward becoming a socialist, centrally-planned, state.

The Banking Institutions

Another indicator of consolidation can be found in our banking institutions. In 1940 there were 14,399 banks in the United States. Today there are about half that many, and the number continues to drop precipitously.[2] A small bank used to be a fixture in the local community; bankers knew their customers by name. Today, small banks are bought out by larger banks more often than not as a way to increase the latter's market share and profits. As banks take on more and more debt to finance their own growth, they make their customers liable for their failure.

And because the FDIC (Federal Deposit Insurance Corporation) is massively in debt, the government's ability to insure and protect depositors' assets is increasingly suspect. The FDIC paid out $36 billion to customers of failed banks in 2009—twice the payout in 2008. More and more of the money in America is being shifted into the hands of fewer and fewer people—banks and government.

Financial Regulation

In April 2010 President Obama sent a financial regulatory bill to Congress designed to end the "too big to fail" phenomenon of 2008—keeping banks from needing and receiving billions of dollars of bailout money in the future. Beneath the rhetoric of necessity and public protection, there can be little doubt that financial regulation is another way in which big government intends to become even bigger.

The Stock Market

In early May 2010 the stock market experienced what is being called a "flash crash"—a massive loss of value (nearly 1000 points on the Dow Index) in a matter of a few hours. No one has been able to identify the cause—some speculated a trader error: typing "billion" instead of "million" in an order entry, causing computers to immediately begin automated selling. While the Dow regained most of the loss by the end of the day, the roller coaster ride caused great panic on Wall Street and Main Street throughout the nation. Could the fall and rise of the market that day have been intentional?

There are many who believe the United States stock and commodities exchanges are no longer free markets—that they are controlled by government agencies and heads of top Wall Street banks. For instance, the government can purchase huge numbers of stock index futures contacts, giving the appearance to observers that the market is gaining new confidence which will, in turn, encourage others to invest. I have no evidence that this is true, but such power is certainly available.

We can study an example from Scripture that illustrates what happens when power is invested in the hands of a single individual.

THE FAMINE FORECAST

The Book of Genesis contains an early record of crisis and consolidation—the story of God using Joseph to save his family (the fledgling nation of Israel) and Egypt from starvation. Note the outline of Joseph's story: He was the second-youngest of his father's 12 sons—and the favorite. His brothers' jealousy caused them to sell Joseph into slavery, and he ended up in Egypt where he became the slave of Potiphar, a ruler who was the equivalent of a modern chief of police. Joseph was falsely accused of a crime and thrown into Pharaoh's royal prison. When Pharaoh had a dream he couldn't interpret, a former jail mate of Joseph's remembered his ability to interpret dreams and recommended that Pharaoh call Joseph.

When Joseph appeared before Pharaoh, he interpreted the dream: There would be seven years of plenty in the land, followed by seven years of famine. But he also gave Pharaoh a plan: Store up 20 percent of the harvest during the abundant years so there would be food available in the famine years. So Pharaoh put Joseph in charge of executing the plan, making him second in authority to Pharaoh himself. Joseph went from a teenager to a slave to a prisoner to the second most important person in the most powerful country in the world.

Joseph's Plan for Centralized Government

There is no record in Scripture of Joseph paying Egyptian farmers for the 20 percent of the grain the government took from them. It was apparently an example of a government deciding by fiat what was required of its citizens and then enforcing the collection.

After the seven years of plenty, seven years of famine began just as Joseph had predicted. The famine was over all the land; all the surrounding nations suffered, "but in the land of Egypt there was bread" (Genesis 41:54). Thanks to Joseph's centralized planning scheme, there was grain for the people to eat. But, even though Joseph had taken the Egyptian's grain without compensation, he charged them for it during the seven years of famine. In fact, when the citizens ran out of money to buy grain, they mortgaged their land to the government in order to pay for the grain.

Joseph's Plan for Survival

As the famine grew worse and more prolonged, the Egyptians realized that Joseph and the government were their only hope. They submitted to him regardless of the cost. They had no money and no hope, so they submitted to Joseph's terms for purchasing grain. Joseph consolidated everything in the land under his control in five different ways:

The Consolidation of the Egyptians' Livelihood

Joseph gathered up all the money to be found in Egypt and brought it into Pharaoh's treasury (Genesis 47:13-14). The Egyptians no longer had any money since they had spent everything they had to buy grain. The government owned all the wealth in the land.

The Consolidation of the Egyptians' Livestock

Next, the people brought their livestock to Joseph in exchange for grain (Genesis 47:15-16). Eventually, everyone in Egypt was reduced to the same level of poverty: no money, no livestock. In bartering grain for livestock, Pharaoh and Joseph brought the people even further under their control and made them even more dependent on government. Livestock in Joseph's day was like a factory today—a capital investment and means of production. When they turned their livestock over to Joseph, Egypt became like a modern communist state—owning the means of production.

The Consolidation of the Egyptians' Land

But it got worse. When the people gave up their capital they were left with nothing but land and themselves. They came to Joseph and offered their land and themselves to the government in exchange for grain. The people were now servants of the state, totally dependent on Joseph to find new ways to let them purchase grain for their families (Genesis 47:18-20).

The Consolidation of the Egyptians' Location

Next, Joseph relocated the people from their relinquished lands into the cities "from one end of the borders of Egypt to the other end" (Genesis 47:21).

We learned in Genesis chapter 41 that during the booming years, Joseph had stored Egypt's grain harvest in the cities. "He laid up in every city the food of the fields which surrounded them" (Genesis 41:48). Since the fields were barren and useless during the years of famine, Joseph eliminated transportation and distribution problems by moving the people to locations where the food was stored.

The Consolidation of the Egyptians' Labor

"Then Joseph said to the people, "Indeed I have bought you and your land this day for Pharaoh. Look, here is seed for you, and you shall sow the land. And it shall come to pass in the harvest that you shall give one-fifth to Pharaoh. Four-fifths shall be your own, as seed for the field and for your food, for those of your households and as food for your little ones" (Genesis 47:23-24).

As the famine was ending, Joseph put the people back to work planting seed in anticipation of the return of the land's fertility. Now, however, they were working by the government's direction on government-owned land and distributing their harvest according to government directives. All control of every aspect of the people's economic lives had been consolidated under the power of Pharaoh.

Was Joseph a Hero or a Tyrant?

Was Joseph a hero, or a government bureaucrat, or maybe even a dictator? He obviously saved Egypt from ruin over a 14-year period by storing up food for seven years in preparation for the coming seven-year famine. But he also consolidated all the wealth, capital, land, and labor in Egypt under the ownership of the government. The people were alive, but they were now beholden to the state for everything. And the New Testament continually presents Joseph as a hero of the faith (Acts 7:9-10; Hebrews 11:22). Two factors will help us resolve the tension we feel about Joseph's goals and the means he used to achieve them.

First, consider the times in which Joseph lived. There was no such thing as democracy or a republican form of government (like America) where individual rights are prominent. Societies were run by strong kings and rulers. And Henry Morris has shown that the 20 percent "tax" imposed by Joseph in the good years was not excessive.[3] We should be so fortunate as to pay only 20 percent of our income in taxes today!

Second, Joseph's actions, extreme as they might seem to us today, were crucial in advancing God's plan for His people, Joseph's family (the family of Jacob, the grandson of Abraham). By sending Joseph to Egypt many years ahead of the need, Joseph was able to create a safe haven for his family, not only to avoid the famine and possible extermination, but to multiply over the next 400 years into a nation that could inherit Canaan, the Promised Land. Therefore, Joseph's actions should be viewed not so much in terms of the Egyptians but in terms of Jacob and his family. God used the nation of Egypt as a resource for the survival of His own chosen people.

Joseph's consolidation of everything in Egypt, extreme as it might seem to us today, is understandable in light of the culture of the day and God's purposes.

The Long-Term Result of Power Consolidation

Joseph's short-term consolidation of power in a time of crisis led to long-term tyranny and judgment by God for Egypt. And the same thing could happen to a nation today that consolidates power for long-term purposes.

Sacrificing Tomorrow on the Altar of Today

Consolidation always becomes a liability in the long run. The power consolidated by Joseph passed to new pharaohs who used it to afflict Israel. Once power is consolidated in the hands of a few, it is very difficult to take back unless there is a revolt. People are often willing to yield their rights to the government to solve a crisis, not realizing it will lead to domination down the road. We may be seeing the same thing happening in our nation, giving the government more power that could lead to slavery in the future.

Submitting the Good of Many to the Control of One

Communism was the great scourge of the twentieth century. Rulers like Stalin, Mao Tse-Tung, and Pol Pot massacred tens of millions of innocent people in order to consolidate power under their leadership. It is estimated that 230 million citizens of these and other totalitarian regimes were killed in the last century alone.[4] We have not reached that point in the U.S.—where one man has that kind of power. But there is no question that more and more power has been consolidated in the hands of the federal government since our nation's founding. And history has proven that most leaders, given the opportunity, will allow the consolidation of power to turn into tyranny.

Our nation is in crisis—financially, ecologically, morally, and spiritually. We must guard against the temptation of granting long-term control in exchange for short-term security.

Notes:

1. Erwin Lutzer, *When A Nation Forgets God - 7 Lessons We Must Learn From Nazi Germany* (Chicago: Moody Press, 2010), 47.

2. "ABC's of Banking," State of Connecticut Department of Banking, *CT.gov*, http://www.ct.gov/DOB/cwp/view.asp?a=2235&q=297892 , (accessed 17 March 2010).

3. Henry M. Morris, *The Genesis Record* (Grand Rapids: Baker Books , 1976), 641.

4. Mark Kramer, et al, Jonathan Murphy, translator, *The Black Book of Communism* (Cambridge, MA: Harvard University Press, 1999), 133-135.

APPLICATION

1. Read Genesis 45:1-18.

   a. How did Joseph get to Egypt in the first place? (verse 4)

   b. Why was Joseph not bitter at his brothers? What perspective did he have on this "unfortunate" circumstance? (verses 5, 8)

   c. How committed was Joseph to what he believed was the plan of God for Egypt and his family? (verses 6-7)

   d. How did Joseph view the role God had given him in Egypt— for his own glory or for the good of his family? (verse 8)

   e. What provision did Joseph and Pharaoh make for Joseph's family? (verses 10, 18; 47:11)

f. What was the result of Jacob's family's sojourn in Egypt? (Genesis 47:27) How did this correspond to God's plan for the descendants of Abraham? (See Genesis 15:5; 17:2.)

g. What cultural fact resulted in Jacob's family settling in an isolated region of Egypt? (See Genesis 43:32; 46:34.) How did this help maintain the purity of Israel as a race descended from Abraham?

2. How complete was the level of power Joseph had in Egypt? (Genesis 41:41-44)

a. What is the difference between God's power and human power? What causes human power to have negative results?

b. What is the best way to ensure human power and authority remains a positive force?

3. Read Acts 7:9-19.

   a. In Stephen's summary, who gets the credit for Joseph's rise to power in Egypt? (verses 9-10)

   b. What does verse 17 indicate about the Jewish understanding of why Jacob's family was sent into Egypt?

   c. What does it say about there being no mention by Stephen about Joseph's consolidation of power in Egypt?

   d. How did that consolidation of power become a negative for Israel after Joseph's death? (verses 18-19)

4. From Joseph's experience, what lesson can you learn about...

   a. Why people are willing to give up their freedom.

b. What rulers should and should not do with their power.

c. The dangers of your nation giving too much power to its leaders.

DID YOU KNOW?

There are many forms of government in which part or all of a nation's power and resources are consolidated in the government: *social-democracy* advocates using the tools of democracy to transition to a socialist state; *socialism* is often viewed as the transitional phase between capitalism and communism; *communism* allows the state government to be in complete control of the economy and the means of production toward the end of all property being shared equally by the people; *fascism/dictatorship* allows one individual to have complete control over a society and to maintain it by terror and strength; *totalitarianism* puts the state in the place of God, subordinating any individual preference to the will of the state.

Satan's CEO

2 Thessalonians 2:1-13

In this lesson we discover the character of the coming Antichrist, and when he will appear.

OUTLINE

Given the dark figures that have appeared in human history, it is hard to imagine one still darker who is yet to appear. He will be the personification of the devil on earth—empowered by Satan to wage final war against God and His people. But like Satan, the fate of the Antichrist is sealed.

I. **The Coming of the Antichrist**
   A. He Cannot Be Revealed Until After the Rapture of the Church
   B. He Cannot Be Revealed Until After the Rejection of the Truth
   C. He Cannot Be Revealed Until After the Holy Spirit Is Removed

II. **The Resume of the Antichrist**
   A. He Will Be a Dynamic Leader
   B. He Will Be Defiant
   C. He Will Be Deceitful
   D. He Will Be Diabolical
   E. He Will Be a Dramatic Leader
   F. He Will Be Demanding
   G. He Will Be Defeated
   H. He Will Be Doomed

The CEO of a corporation or organization is the one responsible for executing the plans approved by the board of directors. In a spiritual sense, Satan is the chairman of the board of evil, and the Antichrist—the human representation of Satan's kingdom on earth who will rise to prominence at the end of the age—is his CEO.

Daniel the prophet was given a revelation (Daniel 8:23-26) of a king who would arise in the "latter times" who would be fierce, powerful, persuasive, and prosperous, who would attack God's "holy people" and destroy many, who would rise up against God himself, who would ultimately be broken "without human means." That is the Antichrist who is yet to come. He will hold sway over the earth during the coming Tribulation, acting as a pseudo-Christ —one who both opposes and imitates Christ at the same time.

Every New Testament use of the word "Antichrist" is by the apostle John in his letters (1 John 2:18, 22; 4:3; 2 John 7). He seems to say that there is an anti-Christ "spirit" that is present in his age and every age, sowing seeds against Jesus Christ, preparing the way for the literal Antichrist at the end of the age. The Antichrist is a person who will appear in the flesh at a certain time, but Satan, who empowers the Antichrist, is alive and well now, doing the work of the Antichrist in preparation for his appearance (2 Thessalonians 2:7).

THE COMING OF THE ANTICHRIST
(2 THESSALONIANS 2:1-7)

In 2 Thessalonians 2, Paul addresses the issue of when the Antichrist will be revealed. Three things have to happen first.

He Cannot Be Revealed Until After the Rapture of the Church (2 Thessalonians 2:1-2)

The church in Thessalonica had been influenced by false teachers who told them the persecution they were enduring was the Tribulation, meaning the Rapture of the Church had already occurred. Paul corrects their misunderstanding and tells them not to believe any such message they receive "by spirit or by word or by letter, as if from us" (verse 2). In Paul's first letter to them he outlined the order of events of the Rapture (1 Thessalonians 4:16-17); and here he reassures them that they are on schedule. Instead of "rapture," Paul refers to "our gathering together to Him"—a perfect description of the event!

The Antichrist cannot be revealed until the Rapture takes place, and the Rapture has not yet occurred. He could be alive on planet earth at this moment, but he hasn't been "revealed" (verse 3) publicly; no one knows who he is.

He Cannot Be Revealed Until After the Rejection of the Truth (2 Thessalonians 2:3a)

Paul says the Thessalonians are not in the Tribulation because it will not come until there is a "falling away" from the truth. "The falling away" is a translation of *apostasia* from which we get "apostasy" —a denial of the truth. "The" is important—it is a prophesied event that will be recognized as a major point of apostasy among professing believers. The Antichrist will not be revealed (made known) until this "falling away" and the Rapture both occur. The apostasy may be sparked by difficult times for Christians prior to the beginning of the Tribulation or by false prophets arising and leading people astray. Whatever the cause, it will be a time when many Christians go back on their profession of faith in Jesus (Matthew 24:10-12; 2 Timothy 4:3-4; 2 Peter 3:3-4).

It's easy to look around in our culture and see how apostasy could begin. We live in an age of "church lite"—where it doesn't cost much to be a Christian. The majority of people who call themselves Christians today just go to church on Sunday morning, if then. How much pressure would it take for them to give up that small commitment? Not very much, I'm afraid. So as persecution heats up in the latter days an apostasy is entirely predictable. In my four decades as a pastor, I have never seen a time when biblical truth and history are more discounted than they are today—even by some who profess to be Christians. I'm afraid the rebuke issued by Christ to the Church at Laodicea could well be aimed at today's church as well: "You are lukewarm" (Revelation 3:15-17).

While some Christians hope to see a worldwide biblical revival just before the return of Christ, I don't see evidence for that in Scripture. Paul clearly describes a great "falling away," not a revival. God could send a revival in His sovereign way, but the Scriptures do not foretell it.

He Cannot Be Revealed Until After the Removal of the Holy Spirit (2 Thessalonians 2:6-7)

The Antichrist cannot be revealed until the Holy Spirit is removed from the earth, allowing all "hell" to break loose on the planet.

Most English Bibles capitalize "He" in verse 7 as a recognition of the fact that "He" refers to the Holy Spirit—the "restrainer." The Holy Spirit is throughout the earth in the lives of true Christian believers, indwelling the Body of Christ which is the Church. It is the presence of the Spirit in the lives of believers and through the Church by which evil is restrained (held back) in the world. He convicts the world "of sin, and of righteousness, and of judgment" (John 16:8). That is the Holy Spirit's three-fold role in the world, accomplishing all three through the Church. When the believers, the Church, are raptured off the earth, the indwelling Spirit will be gone as well. His work of restraining evil (convicting the world) will be finished.

As bad as things seem to be in our world now, imagine what it will be like when Christians and the Holy Spirit are gone! No more salt and light, and no more restraint on sin. All of that will vanish one day in the twinkling of an eye (1 Corinthians 15:52). It's no wonder the Tribulation will begin! The Spirit will be at work during the Tribulation, but in a different way. People will become Christians during that period, and His ministry to them will be active, but perhaps more similar to the Old Testament saints—coming on them rather than dwelling in them.

So, three things must happen before the Antichrist is revealed: the Rapture, the great apostasy, and the removal of the Holy Spirit.

THE RESUME OF THE ANTICHRIST
(2 THESSALONIANS 2:3C-4, 8A, 9-12C)

Scripture provides enough information about the Antichrist to build a picture of his character and activity.

He Will Be a Dynamic Leader

Daniel tells us the Antichrist will speak pompous words directed against God (Daniel 7:8, 25), a characteristic John also records in Revelation 13:5. That should come as no surprise since the Antichrist is the public and human mouthpiece for Satan himself. Whatever you would expect Satan to say about God (as the father of lies, John 8:44), you can also expect the Antichrist to say. He will no doubt be eloquent, a charismatic communicator with the same oratorical skills as Lincoln, Churchill, John F. Kennedy, and Martin Luther King, each of whom could capture an audience with their own personal style. Perhaps Adolf Hitler would be a more apt comparison.

Author A. W. Pink has written,

So it will be with this daring counterfeiter. He will have a mouth speaking very great things. He will have perfect command and flow of language. His oratory will not only gain attention, but respect. Revelation 13:2 declares that his mouth is "as the mouth of a lion" which is a symbolic expression telling of the majesty and awe-producing effects of his voice. The voice of a lion excels that of all other beasts, so the Antichrist will outrival orators both ancient and modern.[1]

He Will Be Defiant

The Antichrist will be defiance, arrogance, and boastfulness personified. He will defy any and every god worshipped by human beings, but especially the God of Israel, his primary target of persecution. He will make no acknowledgement of God, elevating himself above deity in every way (Daniel 11:36-37). He will sit in the temple of God to show that he is God himself (2 Thessalonians 2:3-4).

Obviously, the Jewish temple will have been rebuilt by that day with the Jews living in Israel and in Jerusalem. The latter step was fulfilled in 1948, but the temple remains yet to be reconstructed. In the middle of the Tribulation, the Antichrist will bring an end to sacrifices and offerings and "on the wing of abominations" will he desecrate the temple (Daniel 9:27). Mark 13:14 says that when that abomination takes place, it is time to flee Jerusalem. All on the earth who have not come to know Christ during the Tribulation will "worship him" (Revelation 13:8).

He Will Be Deceitful

In 2 Thessalonians 2:9, Paul refers to the Antichrist as "the lawless one" who operates with "all power, signs, and lying wonders." The triumvirate of power, signs, and wonders was first used to describe the supernatural ministry of Jesus. Jesus' miracles were true miracles, as opposed to the lying miracles of the Antichrist. Yes, the Antichrist will work miracles, but not by the power of God. They will be counterfeit miracles worked to deceive the naïve into believing the Antichrist is from God.

And many will believe the Antichrist's lies (2 Thessalonians 2:10-12). There will be many saved during the Tribulation, but many also who will not. As for those who reject the Gospel all their lives and enter the Tribulation as unbelievers, will they be able to be saved?

The best evidence suggests that they will not be saved; that because of their steadfast rejection of the truth when they had the opportunity, they will reap the results of their choice and suffer under "strong delusion, that they should believe the lie" (verse 11). While I can't prove that I'm right with that interpretation, I know I wouldn't take a chance. Many people are putting off salvation today, hoping for a second chance that the Bible nowhere offers. Today is the day to be saved (2 Corinthians 6:2).

He Will Be Diabolical

During the Tribulation, the Antichrist will: persecute Christians; kill two heaven-sent witnesses to the Gospel; lead the nations against Jerusalem; and set his sights on eliminating the Jewish people. Does that sound diabolical?

He will make a covenant with Israel at the beginning of the Tribulation—a peace treaty, promising to protect them from their attackers. But halfway through the promised seven-year treaty period the Antichrist will break his covenant and turn all his satanic rage and hatred directly toward Israel. That is when he creates an abomination in the Holy of Holies in the temple in Jerusalem, desecrating the most holy site in Judaism. It is this kind of diabolical trickery that makes the Antichrist a true son of his lying father, the devil.

With that act of treachery, the countdown to Armageddon begins.

He Will Be a Dramatic Leader

Revelation 13 tells the amazing story of the Antichrist suffering a mortal wound and coming back to life! This will do nothing but elevate his status in the eyes of the world's deceived population and give credence to his claims of deity. This act is nothing more than an attempt to discredit the death and resurrection of Jesus Christ. I do not personally believe it will be an actual resurrection, but it will appear that he was dead and came back to life—another of his lying "signs and wonders." Real or not, the people of the world who see this "miracle" on globe-spanning video will believe it to be real. And they will worship the Antichrist.

He Will Be a Demanding Leader

The Antichrist will require everyone in the world to receive the "mark of the beast," a sign of loyalty to him, on their hand or forehead in order to engage in commerce—to buy or sell the necessities of life (Revelation 13:17). Imagine not being able to go to the store to buy what your family needs without receiving the mark of Satan's CEO on your body. There will be many who will be cowed into submission out of fear of punishment or death. Others, loyal to Christ, may starve to death because of the inability to purchase food. This kind of demanding allegiance should make it clear to all—whether they resist him or not—exactly what kind of heartless leader the Antichrist is.

He Will Be a Defeated Leader

The only just end for someone like the Antichrist is for him to be defeated by God—and he will be. His end is preceded by the global conflagration known as Armageddon, where the Antichrist unites the world's armies against Israel but is defeated by the returning Christ and the armies of heaven. By the force of Christ's judgment, the boastful mouth of the Antichrist is closed forever (Revelation 19:19-20).

He Will Be Doomed

Both the Old and New Testaments provide clear evidence of the final end of the Antichrist: "I watched till the beast was slain, and its body destroyed and given to the burning flame" (Daniel 7:11); "[The beast and false prophet] were cast alive into the lake of fire burning with brimstone" (Revelation 19:20). The Antichrist will have his way for seven years, then God will have His way for all eternity. Interestingly, the beast and his deputy, the false prophet, are cast into hell ahead of Satan, who is not dispatched until the end of the Millennium, a thousand years after the other two arrive.

A Seleucid king named Antiochus Epiphanes reigned in the period between the Testaments, prior to the birth of Christ, and serves as an Old Testament picture of the Antichrist. He was a violent, wicked king—especially in his persecution of the Jews of that day. On one occasion, when Antiochus was defeated in a battle with the Egyptians, the Jews in Jerusalem celebrated when they received word of his defeat. So he returned to Jerusalem and slaughtered thousands of Jews out of pure anger.

A Jewish priest named Mattathias, along with his son, led an uprising against Antiochus—a guerilla war, inflicting great damage on Antiochus' armies. Through the leadership of Mattathias and his army, the temple was recaptured and cleansed; and the celebration of Hanukkah, or Feast of Dedication, was instituted as a commemoration (see John 10:22-23). Having enough oil to light the menorah for only one day, legend says that the oil miraculously lasted all eight days of the feast—a miracle celebrated by Jews today as Hanukkah.

Even in the darkest of days, God provides light. And even when things look their darkest in the days ahead, especially during the Tribulation and the Antichrist's reign of terror, we can be guided by the light of the revelation that Christ will return to establish His eternal kingdom. Hallelujah!

Note:

1. A. W. Pink, *The Antichrist* (Grand Rapids: Kregel Publishing, 1988), 9.

1. What do the two references to the Antichrist in 2 Thessalonians 2:3 indicate about this man?

    a. "man of sin"

    b. "the son of perdition"

    c. How about "lawless one" in verse 8?

2. How do you think it will be possible for the Antichrist to gain such worldwide allegiance?

    a. What does that say about peoples' desire to find answers in human leaders?

b. Since the Antichrist could be on the world political stage (but not identified) prior to the Rapture, what will keep you from leaning toward him? What defenses will keep you from being deceived by him?

c. What have you learned in this chapter about the slow, subtle process of shifts in power? Do you see that occurring in your country? If so, where?

3. What traits do you expect to find in a society growing more apostate in the end times? (Matthew 24:10-12)

a. To what do "itching ears" refer in 2 Timothy 4:3?

b. What do people do when they grow weary of "sound doctrine"? (verse 3) What does "heap up" mean with regard to teachers?

c. How would you define a "scoffer" based on their words in
2 Peter 3:3-4?

d. Why is it dangerous to listen to scoffers? How can Satan use
their mocking in the mind of a Christian?

4. Read Revelation 13:1-17.

a. Who gives the Antichrist his power and authority? (verse 2;
see Revelation 12 also)

b. How long will the Antichrist's authority last? (verse 5)
What is this length in years? (See Daniel 9:27.)

c. Describe the kind of power he will have during that period.
(verses 6-7)

d. How will Christians be different from non-Christians during
that period? (verse 8)

e. How would you interpret the meaning of verses 9-10?

f. How will Christians overcome the pressure against them during the Tribulation? (Revelation 12:11)

g. What would you do if you could not purchase food for your family without receiving the mark of the beast? (verses 16-17)

DID YOU KNOW?

The English word "antichrist" is made up of two Greek words: *anti* (against; instead of) and *christos* (anointed one, Messiah, Christ). Therefore, "antichrist" can be interpreted as one who acts against Christ or who acts instead of (in place of, as a counterfeit) Christ. Interestingly, the biblical Antichrist plays both roles: an opponent and an imposter; a satanic counterfeit of the true Christ. Though the biblical Antichrist is referred to by more than 25 different names in Scripture, the word Antichrist appears only four times in Scripture: 1 John 2:18, 22: 4:3; 2 John 7. Though there will be "the" Antichrist at the end of the age, everyone empowered by Satan to lie about God and Christ and oppose the spread of God's kingdom is referred to by John as an "antichrist" (small "a," 1 John 2:18, 22).

THE MARK OF THE BEAST

Revelation 13:1-18

In this lesson we learn about the satanic activity of the Antichrist and the False Prophet during the Tribulation.

OUTLINE

If a well-known political leader today suddenly began manifesting miraculous powers—signs and wonders—he would receive instant acclaim. During the Tribulation, Satan will give such power to the Antichrist and False Prophet to induce the world to worship them instead of God.

I. **The Mark Is Originated by Satan**

II. **The Mark Is Ordered by the Antichrist**

III. **The Mark Is Orchestrated by the False Prophet**
   A. The Description of the False Prophet
   B. The Deeds of the False Prophet
   C. The Deception of the False Prophet
   D. The Demand of the False Prophet
   E. The Doom of the False Prophet and His Followers

October 7, 2009, marked the fifty-seventh anniversary of the barcode—that rectangular set of black lines on a white background that appears on everything we purchase today. Officially known as a UPC—Universal Product Code—the barcode was invented by two American graduate students and first used at a supermarket in Troy, Ohio, in 1974.

While the barcode is not going away, a new identification system—RFID (Radio Frequency IDentification)—is becoming even more widespread. It is a tiny microchip that is used to keep track of products in shipment, the movement of people (via a chip on a name or ID tag), even animals. RFID chips are everywhere—and usually unseen because of their tiny size. And the technology is now available to implant the chips, about the size of a grain of rice, under human skin. Their first use is to implant them under the skin of emergency workers, soldiers, and others to make identification possible as a last resort.

While fascinating, this technology is frightening at the same time, especially to those who have read Revelation 13—a chapter detailing some of the policies of the Antichrist during the Tribulation. We are already seeing a gradual erosion of privacy in our day, and during the Tribulation citizens will have none. When we look at where technology is taking us, we can only stand in awe of the biblical prophecies made 1,900 years ago depicting these same events. God knows the beginning and the end, seeing past, present, and future as one (Isaiah 46:9-10). The mark of the beast, the subject of this lesson, is a prime example of how biblical prophecy will be fulfilled with today's technology.

I am often asked whether Christians, who will be raptured from the earth before the Tribulation, need to be concerned about these developments. We know the events of Revelation 13 take place in the second half of the seven-year Tribulation, or three-and-one-half years after the Rapture of the Church. We also know that the Rapture is imminent—that it could happen at any moment. No other biblical prophecy needs to be fulfilled before the Rapture can occur. So if the Rapture could happen today, then we could be just three or four years away from the events described in Revelation 13. But those events will not happen suddenly. There will be a gradual buildup to those events. And we are living in a time when the technology is developing and the sweeping power of government is growing to the extent that we could begin to see signs of the nearness of the Tribulation events taking place. I truly believe we are living in the shadows of Tribulation events.

Revelation 13 introduces us to the methods for population control the Antichrist will use in the second half of the Tribulation, one of them being a "mark" affixed to the hand or forehead of every individual on earth.

THE MARK IS ORIGINATED BY SATAN (REVELATION 13:2)

We are told in verse 2 that it is "the dragon" which gives "the beast" (the Antichrist) his power. The reference to Satan as "the dragon" comes from the previous chapter, Revelation 12:9, which depicts "the great dragon" being cast out of heaven along with the rebellious angels who were allied with him. It is obvious in Revelation 12 that the dragon is Satan. And in Revelation 13, John continues by saying it is the dragon who empowers the beast (the Antichrist).

It is Satan's desire to be worshipped that we see also in the Antichrist. In Isaiah 14:12-14 we find Satan saying, "I will be like the Most High" (verse 14). And when Satan tempted Jesus in the wilderness, he offered Jesus "all the kingdoms of the world" if Jesus would "fall down and worship [him]" (Matthew 4:8-9). It is Satan's long-standing desire to be worshiped "like the Most High," and it is no surprise that we have seen an increase in Satan worship in our day. And his primary goal during the Tribulation will be to deflect worship away from the true and living God to his (Satan's) representative on earth, the Antichrist.

Satan is a counterfeiter; a copycat. We'll see that just as God is a Trinity, Satan has his own trinity: himself, the Antichrist, and the False Prophet. Just as the Holy Spirit brings glory to Jesus Christ, so the False Prophet will bring glory to the Antichrist. The mark of the beast is a way to force people to worship someone out of fear.

THE MARK IS ORDERED BY THE ANTICHRIST (REVELATION 13:1-10)

John saw the beast rising up out of the sea. The beast is a composite of the four animals seen by Daniel in his prophecy of the end times. They represented Babylon, Medo-Persia, Greece, and Rome. The beast has seven heads and 10 horns and represents the ruler of the revived Roman Empire, the Antichrist himself. He will be an international leader, uniting people from all races and all regions of the world. No human could do that alone, but with Satan working behind the scenes, it will happen.

The Antichrist's activities are detailed in verses 3-10, activities that are consistent with Satan's career—especially the Antichrist's blasphemous words against God. Satan's main mission in life is to make God look bad so people will not worship Him. And the Antichrist will take up that blasphemous task during his time on earth with the intent to turn people away from God to worship him.

He also makes war against the saints—those who profess faith in Christ during the Tribulation. He exercises power over "every tribe, tongue, and nation" (verse 7). And he is successful: "All who dwell on the earth will worship him"—all, that is, "whose names have not been written in the Book of Life of the Lamb slain from the foundation of the world" (verse 8). A frightening world is coming shortly.

THE MARK IS ORCHESTRATED BY THE FALSE PROPHET (REVELATION 13:11-18)

The mark is originated with Satan and ordered by the Antichrist, but it is orchestrated by the False Prophet—the second beast of Revelation 13. He is the one who executes the plan to put the mark of the beast on the population of planet earth.

The Description of the False Prophet (Revelation 13:11-12)

John notes that this second beast looks like a lamb but speaks like a dragon. That is, he appears meek and mild but, in reality, is bent on destruction. Again, Satan is all about counterfeiting. Jesus was "the Lamb of God who takes away the sin of the world" (John 1:29), so Satan makes the False Prophet into a false lamb. But this lamb is really a wolf in sheep's clothing; a demonized man exercising authority and power in the name of the Antichrist. He has miraculous powers by which he amazes and deceives the residents of planet earth (verses 13-14).

Though Christians will not be around to witness these miracles, we must beware of False Prophets today who are "ravenous wolves" in sheep's clothing (Matthew 7:15). Many could be named, but Jim Jones (The Peoples Temple) is a good example—a preacher who began his ministry based on Scripture but ultimately led hundreds of people to their deaths by suicide in Guyana. This tragic case of satanic deception ended in the deaths of hundreds of hopeful, but deceived, people.

The Deeds of the False Prophet
(Revelation 13:13)

I fear some Christians underestimate the power of our enemy. He gives the False Prophet power to work miracles—"great signs" —like making "fire come down from heaven on the earth in the sight of men." Satan is not God's peer or equal. But he is definitely powerful and can create "signs" that look equivalent to what God has done. Again, his expertise is counterfeiting.

The reason the False Prophet calls down fire from heaven is probably a reference to Malachi 4:5-6 which says that before the coming of the Messiah, Elijah will appear. And Elijah is the only Old Testament prophet to have called down fire from heaven. The False Prophet will be attempting to convince people he is Elijah— the forerunner of the Lord who will return. It is a deceitful attempt to give an air of legitimacy to his presence.

The Deception of the False Prophet
(Revelation 13:14-15)

The False Prophet's miracles have their intended effect: he convinces people to build "an image to the beast"—a giant image in honor of the Antichrist (verse 14). I believe the Antichrist then sets this image in the rebuilt Jewish temple in Jerusalem, in the Holy of Holies, thus fulfilling the prophecy of Daniel 12:11 (also in Daniel 9:27 and 11:31) concerning "the abomination of desolation." This prophecy of Daniel was fulfilled as a foreshadowing by Antiochus Epiphanes who set up a statue of the Greek god Zeus in the Holy of Holies and sacrificed a pig on the temple altar. These acts would have indeed been an abomination to any God-fearing Jew of the day. And the Antichrist will perform similar acts with the help of the False Prophet.

Jesus also made reference to this coming abomination in Matthew 24:15-16, 21. This act marks the beginning of the second half of the Tribulation (see the 1,290 days, or three-and-one-half years mentioned in Daniel 12:11). Following this event, Jesus said, "there will be great tribulation, such as has not been since the beginning of the world until this time" (Matthew 24:21).

At the beginning of the Tribulation, the Antichrist will make a covenant with Israel to protect her against her enemies. But he breaks the covenant at the midpoint of the Tribulation and turns against

Israel by desecrating her temple and Holy of Holies. He defiles everything the Jews hold holy and turns his full fury upon Israel to destroy her. Paul says that the Antichrist will "sit as God in the temple of God, showing himself that he is God" (2 Thessalonians 2:4). At that moment, the diabolical trinity of Satan, the Antichrist, and the False Prophet have fulfilled their desire of receiving worship as God.

And here is a truly diabolical part: The False Prophet is able to cause the image of the Antichrist to speak (Revelation 13:15). There is no magic or deceit here. It is pure demonic power at work according to the testimony of 2 Thessalonians 2:9: "The coming of the lawless one is according to the working of Satan, with all power, signs, and lying wonders." Satan has the power to make an inanimate object like an image appear to come to life. It is another example of the dark power that will characterize the Tribulation period—especially the second half.

The Demand of the False Prophet
(Revelation 13:16-18)

Once the Antichrist's and False Prophet's power have been displayed, they are ready to demand the acceptance of the mark of the beast "on their right hand or on their foreheads."

Again, counterfeiting is seen. In Revelation 7:3 the servants of God are sealed on their foreheads to set them apart from those not belonging to Him. These are the 144,000 Jewish witnesses who serve as evangelists during the Tribulation period. The seal is to protect them before certain judgments are released on the earth. The Antichrist's seal is for the same purpose: protection. By receiving his mark, people will be able to buy and sell and engage in commerce. Without it, they will become targets of the Antichrist. The RFID microchip already mentioned is a possible way for this to take place.

The Doom of the False Prophet and His Followers (Revelation 19:19-20)

In spite of the power and control the Antichrist exercises during the Tribulation, his doom is sealed. We turn forward in Revelation to chapter 19 for the details. There we find that "these two [the beast and the False Prophet] were cast alive into the lake of fire burning with brimstone" (verse 20).

And those who took the mark of the beast and worshiped his image did not fare well either. Revelation 16:1-2 details "a foul and loathsome sore" that came upon them. Revelation 14:9-11 says they will "drink of the wine of the wrath of God" and "shall be tormented with fire and brimstone in the presence of the holy angels and in the presence of the Lamb . . . forever and ever." While it may appear that those who take the mark of the beast are simply doing what they have to do to protect themselves and their families, they are judged for identifying with the satanic evil of the Antichrist.

What is the mark of the beast? Revelation 13:18 says, "Let him who has understanding calculate the number of the beast, for it is the number of a man. His number is 666." For 1,900 years people have wanted to know what 666 represents, who it points to. People are afraid of the number—to have it in their address or their phone number.

There have been numerous attempts through the years to come up with a mathematical formula for equating letters with numbers in order to arrive at 666 and thus the identity of the Antichrist. But all those attempts have failed. Perhaps the best thing to remember is that the number seven in Scripture is the number of completeness —the divine number. Six, therefore, is an incomplete number, a number that falls short of God's completeness. And human beings certainly fall short of God's completeness due to sin. That may be what 666 represents: incomplete man rebelling against God.

What about those who refuse to take the mark of the beast? Revelation 20:4 identifies them as having been "beheaded for their witness to Jesus and for the word of God," for not worshiping the beast or his image and not receiving the mark of the beast. "And they lived and reigned with Christ for a thousand years." They are resurrected and rule with Christ during the Millennium.

If you are a Christian today, you will never face the decision of whether to receive the mark of the beast or not. You will be in heaven with Christ during the Tribulation. But what would you do if you were faced with such a decision—a decision to swear allegiance to a godless ruler or maintain your allegiance to Christ? We have examples in Scripture of people faced with that choice: Daniel's three friends, Shadrach, Meshach, and Abed Nego. They refused to worship the king of Babylon and were sorely tested—but God preserved them. They didn't know He would. They were willing to die as faithful Jews (Daniel 3).

That should be our stance today as well. Whether we are tested with ridicule, embarrassment, financial reversal, or even the threat of death—may God give us grace to stay true to the One who has given His all to save us for all eternity.

APPLICATION

1. Read Isaiah 14:12-14.

   a. Where was Satan (Lucifer) before being consigned to earth? (verse 12a)

   b. Describe the five prideful assertions Lucifer made that resulted in his downfall: (verses 13-14)

      1) I will _____

      2) I will _____

      3) I will _____

      4) I will _____

      5) I will _____

   c. Which of the five most clearly parallels the intention of the Antichrist during the Tribulation?

2. Read Matthew 7:15-20.

   a. What does Jesus warn His followers about in this passage? (verse 15)

   b. Why does Jesus make this warning? (Is it possible that something can appear legitimate to us when it really isn't?)

   c. How does Paul affirm this possibility in 2 Corinthians 11:13-15?

d. How do the men in Paul's day parallel the activity of the False Prophet during the Tribulation?

e. What does the term "ravenous wolves" in Matthew 7:15 signify to you? (How serious is the intent of False Prophets?)

f. How does Jesus say a False Prophet can be detected? (verse 16)

g. Why are miracles not always the only "fruit" that must be checked? (Revelation 13:13-14)

h. What other kinds of "fruit" should one look for? (Galatians 5:22-23)

i. What is the ultimate determinant of whether a New Testament "prophet" is true or false? (1 John 2:22)

j. If a tree ("prophet") bears some good fruit and some bad fruit, what determination must be made about him? (verses 17-18)

k. What must be done with trees that bear bad fruit? (verse 19) How would you translate this metaphor into practical terms for the church today?

3. Read Daniel 3:16-18.

   a. What were the three Hebrew men convinced God was able to do? (verse 17)

   b. But what did they know might actually happen? (verse 18a)

   c. What difference did it make to them what God chose to do? (verse 18)

   d. Why is it important to decide on our convictions before pressure arises in our life?

DID YOU KNOW?

RFID (Radio Frequency IDentification) tags, like a barcode, require a reader to pull data stored on the RFID microchip. Because the information is transmitted wirelessly, RFID chips have an advantage over barcodes in that they can be read at a distance. RFID tags are currently used to track livestock (chips in ear tags), monitor individuals coming in and out of facilities (employees wearing ID badges with embedded chips), inventory control (chips embedded in clothing and on pallets of products in shipment), transportation payments (cars going through toll booths, passengers boarding buses, subways, and trains), timing of individuals and vehicles in sport races, tracking international travel via passport chips, and many other uses. Human implants of RFID chips have been in progress since 1998.

FINANCIAL SIGNS OF THE END TIMES

Selected Scriptures

In this lesson we note financial trends that are building toward the Tribulation and the end of the age.

OUTLINE

When it comes to money, life today is radically different from just a few decades ago. Today, the financial world operates electronically; wealth is concentrated in the hands of a minority of people; the middle class is vanishing; and oil has become an international bargaining chip.

   I.   **The Proliferation of Global Technology**

  II.   **The Polarization of Prosperity and Poverty**

 III.   **The Priority of Oil and the Middle East**

 IV.   **The Preoccupation With Money and Material Things**

  V.   **The Passive Indifference to the Warnings of God**

We have already discussed the order of end-time events: the Rapture, then the Tribulation, then the Second Coming of Christ, then the Millennium, then the eternal state. And we have said that nothing needs to happen in order for the Rapture to take place—it could happen today. So, if the Rapture occurs just before the Tribulation, and if we see signs of the Tribulation growing more certain, that means the Rapture is getting closer as well.

Those signs include a one world economic system that can eventually be controlled by a one world ruler, the Antichrist. In this lesson we will examine financial signs of the end times to add to the growing body of evidence that the Tribulation (and thus the Rapture) is growing near.

THE PROLIFERATION OF GLOBAL TECHNOLOGY (REVELATION 13:16-17)

In the previous lesson, we studied the mark of the beast that will be one's permission to buy or sell during the Tribulation. A century ago, such a thing would have sounded like science fiction. But now the technology exists to make it a reality. When you pass through a grocery store checkout line, your ability to pay could easily be linked to permission to purchase.

A "cashless" society has been slowly developing, a society where all transactions are handled electronically instead of by currency. This is a necessary part of worldwide commerce, of course—removing the necessity for sending cash (or checks—a hard copy of cash) around the world. And if a person's bank account can be stored electronically, it would be just another step to store complete information on that person as well—such as whether they have permission to buy and sell (that is, whether they have the mark of the beast). These changes happen so slowly, so incrementally, that hardly anyone notices over time. But compare today with 30 years ago and you'll see that a significant line has been crossed. In fact, the day is probably fast approaching when a surcharge may be levied on customers who choose to use cash instead of an electronic medium for purchases. Imagine— penalized for using money!

No money will change hands in the future. Paychecks and other checks will all be deposited electronically as many of them already are. Some are suggesting that physical money may be a way for germs to be transmitted—like flu viruses—providing another reason for the elimination of currency. Since credit and debit cards rarely leave your hand—you swipe your own card now—there's no danger of germ exchange with plastic.

The next major step toward the cashless society is transactions via cell phones. Since the majority of the world now uses cell phones, the infrastructure is in place. It is simply a matter of increasing broadband wireless access and working out the electronic links. In some Asian countries, consumers already use their cell phones (electronic wallets) to make transactions. Cell phones will gradually replace many laptops as the preferred means for accessing the Internet, including electronic financial transactions. Soon, cell phones will have all the capabilities of laptop or desktop computers.

As an addendum, let me mention that with the increase in these technologies come additional opportunities for ministry. At Turning Point, we are working on strategies for disseminating solid Bible teaching via cell phones. We want to take advantage of every technological opportunity to share the Gospel.

THE POLARIZATION OF PROSPERITY AND POVERTY (REVELATION 6:5-6)

Revelation 6-19 covers the time of the Tribulation on earth, so 6:5-6 reflects events early in the Tribulation. These verses describe the opening of the third seal (judgment) and the release of the black horse and rider upon the earth. The rider is holding a pair of scales in his hand, saying, "A quart of wheat for a denarius, and three quarts of barley for a denarius; and do not harm the oil and the wine." This is a picture of worldwide famine, a time when the poor will get poorer and the rich will be living in luxury.

A denarius was a day's wage, so a quart of wheat cost one day's wage. Barley, a cheaper grain, would be three quarts for a denarius. So it would take a day's wages just to buy food for a day, with nothing left over. It is a picture of extreme deprivation on earth for most people. But the hardships will not touch everyone equally.

Verse 6 concludes by saying, "And do not harm the oil and the wine," meaning that while the basic staples will be in short supply, the finer things (oil and wine) will go untouched. Therefore, the average person will suffer while the wealthy do just fine.

We've seen the division between the rich and poor already, most notably in the current financial crisis. Main Street suffered while sometimes Wall Street prospered. The taxpayers bailed out Wall Street banks only to see them reward themselves with huge year-end bonuses—as if the financial crisis never happened.

A 2006 United Nations report showed that, increasingly, the wealth of the world is being consolidated in the hands of a smaller and smaller minority of people. Half the world's population owns barely one percent of global wealth. The top 10 percent of the U. S. population owns 71 percent of U. S. wealth while the bottom 40 percent owns less than one percent of U. S. wealth.[1] There is a massive polarization of wealth taking place in the world. The gap between rich and poor is growing wider day by day.

THE PRIORITY OF OIL AND THE MIDDLE EAST (EZEKIEL 38:10-12)

Ezekiel 38:10-12 deals with a war that I believe will take place in the early days of the seven-year Tribulation. Others see it happening just prior to the Rapture. Either way, it could well be within our lifetime. The war involves a coalition of nations that plans to destroy Israel—and would, except for the intervention of the Lord.

The motivation of the coalition is oil. The Middle East was the site of the Garden of Eden, the site of lush forests that have decayed into the greatest reservoirs of oil on the planet. A geophysicist explained to a good friend of mine how the largest deposits of petroleum in the world lie under the sands in countries just to the east of Israel where the world was once covered by far-reaching forests and plant life like the world has never seen. The oil buried under the surface of the Middle East will become the motivation for wars in the years ahead. Satan could finance the Battle of Armageddon with oil derived from the decaying Garden he helped to ruin at the dawn of human history!

It is a fact that the majority of the world's oil reserves, 75 percent, are controlled by Islamic nations—nations that hate Israel and

America. God is going to use the world hunger for oil to draw the nations of the world into the Middle East for a conflagration: "I will turn you around, put hooks into your jaws, and lead you out, with all your army, horses, and horsemen, all splendidly clothed, a great company with bucklers and shields, all of them handling swords" (Ezekiel 38:4). I believe it is possible, with the place that oil holds in our world's economy, that the stage is being set for just such a gathering of nations.

You've heard the expression, "Follow the money." In the end times, it is going to be "Follow the oil." Oil will represent wealth and mobility, and nations will go to war over it.

THE PREOCCUPATION WITH MONEY AND MATERIAL THINGS (2 TIMOTHY 3:1-5)

Everyone in the world is being, and will be more and more, affected by money and material things. In past generations in America, people lived in farming communities where natural resources— food, land, livestock—played an important role in sustenance. But today, everything revolves around the exchange of money.

In 2 Timothy 3:1-2a, Paul wrote to Timothy to say that "in the last days perilous times will come. For men will be lovers of themselves, lovers of money." Paul lists many characteristics of people in the last days, and one of the first on his list is that people will be lovers of money. It's interesting that the first two—lovers of self and lovers of money—are mentioned together. So often, self-centered and selfish people are also greedy people. There have been many wealthy corporate executives convicted in recent years of defrauding stockholders, employees, and customers. They seemingly had no concerns except for their own accumulation of wealth. Individuals' loss of savings? Investors' loss of capital? Employees' loss of jobs? It didn't matter as long as they grew wealthier. That is the spirit of our age and it will become more pronounced the closer we get to the end of the age.

Sadly, Paul says that some of these people will have "a form of godliness" without its true power. In other words, they will be religious people, even professing Christians. The spirit of the age is not only among pagans; it has, and will, infect the church of Jesus Christ. The love of money is at the core of modern society. Money drives commerce; money is power; money is a measure of worth and self-esteem.

No wonder Paul wrote to Timothy that "the love of money is a root of all kinds of evil, for which some have strayed from the faith" (1 Timothy 6:10). And no wonder Jesus said it is impossible to serve two masters, God and money (Matthew 6:24). Neither Paul nor Jesus said you cannot have money and love God. They just said you cannot love money and God at the same time.

Nothing has dominated the news cycles in our country in recent years more than money—that is, the economy. It is what our society depends on for happiness and well-being.

THE PASSIVE INDIFFERENCE TO THE WARNINGS OF GOD (LUKE 17:26-30)

People today are amazingly indifferent to what God says about the end of the age—even Christians! It's as if what the Bible says is not really meant to inform us, that it is just "Bible language" talking about "something" that really has little to do with me. That is certainly the view of the world, but it is also the view of many Christians.

Luke 17:26-30 is a prophecy from Jesus Christ Himself about "the day when the Son of Man is revealed" (verse 30). Jesus compares that coming generation with the generation that experienced the flood in Noah's day and the destruction of Sodom and Gomorrah in Lot's day. The reference is not to the people's wickedness or debauchery; it is simply to their ordinariness. They were going about business as usual and never saw the judgment that was coming. The verbs Jesus uses say it all: they ate, drank, married, bought, sold, planted, built—they were just living their lives without any awareness of what was happening around them.

One of the biggest challenges preachers have is getting people's attention. People are so caught up in the mundane (but demanding) affairs of their lives that a worship service is more of an opportunity just to sit and rest for an hour than it is to pay attention to the truths of the Word of God. When they leave, things continue on just as they did before they came in. And Jesus said it will be the same way in the end times—which certainly can include our day.

In the letters Christ dictated to the apostle John when he was exiled on the island of Patmos, there are some similar descriptions (Revelation 2-3). The seven churches Christ addressed were literal churches, but I also believe the seven churches are pictures of the stages of the church in the last 1,900 years since Christ. The Laodicean church represents the church on earth prior to the return of Christ to earth (Revelation 3:14-18). About this church (the church in our day) John Stott wrote,

> The Laodicean church was a halfhearted church. . . It describes vividly the respectable, sentimental, nominal, skin-deep religiosity which is so widespread among us today. Our Christianity is flabby and anemic. We appear to have taken a lukewarm bath [in] religion.[2]

If you attend a strong, Bible-believing, Christ-honoring church, you may think that's an overstatement. But not all churches are like yours. There is a large part of professing Christianity that is very nominal—very much like John Stott describes it. They are, to use Christ's words in Revelation, "lukewarm, and neither cold nor hot" (Revelation 3:16).

Jesus said some peoples' hearts will grow cold in the end times (Matthew 24:12), but in Revelation He described hearts that are neither "hot nor cold." A lukewarm heart is a heart that is passively indifferent. It doesn't matter whether they attend church or not: "It doesn't hurt, so why go?"

The cure for the lukewarm church is found in Revelation 3:20 where Jesus is standing at the door of the Laodicean church: "Behold, I stand at the door and knock. If anyone hears My voice and opens the door, I will come in to him and dine with him, and he with Me." While that verse is often used in terms of personal evangelism, its context is the Church. Jesus wants His entire Church to hear His knock and open the door and allow Him to come in. He wants to reclaim His rightful place as the Lord of the church. What a sad indictment of the condition of the church today—that the Lord of the Church needs to ask to enter!

This is a warning and a rebuke not only to Christians but to pastors who are the leaders of local churches. It is just as easy for churches to get caught up in "playing church" as it is for Christians to get caught up in "living life." In any case, Christ and His plan for the ages can be completely ignored and overlooked. No wonder Jesus asked, "Nevertheless, when the Son of Man comes, will He really find faith on the earth?" (Luke 18:8b).

The picture of Christ knocking on the door of His Church was captured famously years ago in a painting by artist Holman Hunt.

Christ is standing outside a door; weeds have grown up around the dwelling. And most notably, there is no handle on the outside of the door! The intent of the artist was clear: Christ will not open the door to the Church or a person's heart by force. The door can only be opened from the inside by the occupant.

Have you opened the door of your heart to Christ? Don't be one of those too busy with the cares of this world to note the changing seasons of the ages. He is coming soon!

Notes:

1. James Randerson, "World's Richest 1% Own 40% of All Wealth, UN Report Discovers," *Guardian News*, 6 December 2006, <http://www.guardian.co.uk/money/2006/dec/06/business.internationalnews> (accessed 28 October 2009).]

2. John Stott, *What Christ Thinks of the Church* (Grand Rapids: Zondervan, 1964), 116.

APPLICATION

1. Read 2 Peter 1:12-21.

   a. What role was Peter playing with those to whom he wrote? (verses 12-13)

   b. What was the source of all that he had taught those he mentored in the faith? (verses 16-18; see Matthew 17:5)

   c. To what "prophetic word" is Peter referring in verse 19?

   d. What metaphor does Peter use about the role of prophetic words in the believer's heart? (verse 19)

   e. To what does the last part of verse 19 refer? What is "the day"? (See 2 Timothy 1:12.)

   f. What comfort do verses 19-20 give the student of the end times as he seeks out God's plans for the near future?

g. How much emphasis do you give in your Bible reading to understanding Scriptures related to the end times?

h. What principles does Proverbs 2:1-5 offer about seeking God's truth?

2. Compare Matthew 6:19-20 with James 5:1-6. What principles were the rich violating?

a. What evidence of a "middle class" do you find in the James passage?

b. What signs do you see in America of a "vanishing" middle class—of the rich getting richer and the poor getting poorer?

3. In what sense could Luke 18:8 have been written about Christ's first coming to earth? (See John 1:11.)

4. Read 2 Timothy 3:1-9.

   a. Write down all the characteristics of those who will populate the "last days."

   b. What does "form of godliness" mean in verse 5?

   c. How do people "deny" the power of godliness? What is the power of godliness? (verse 5)

   d. What command does Paul give Timothy concerning such people? (verse 5b)

   e. What does verse 7 suggest about the danger of "head knowledge" alone when it comes to Scripture?

5. What rebuke did Jesus give to the Pharisees and Sadducees in Matthew 16:1-3?

    a. What positive trait did the sons of Issachar possess? (1 Chronicles 12:32)

    b. What signs of the times are you learning about in this study?

DID YOU KNOW?

The federal government is proposing a national strategy for Americans to conduct online transactions securely and privately without the need for usernames and passwords. The White House has dubbed its proposal, the "Identity Ecosystem." This single authenticated ID could be used to access everything from online health records, and banking information, to email. Howard Schmidt, cybersecurity coordinator and special assistant to the President, blogged that the framework would be user-centric, "That means you, as a user, will be able to have more control of the private information you use to authenticate yourself on-line, and generally will not have to reveal more than is necessary to do so."

FOXBusiness.com "Uncle Sam Wants You to Have an Online ID" and DarkReading.com "White House Cybersecurity Czar Unveils National Strategy for Trusted Online Identity"

THE COLLAPSE OF THE GLOBAL FINANCIAL MARKET

Revelation 18:1-24

In this lesson we see the future revival and destruction of Babylon, the center of the coming world economy.

OUTLINE

When we think of the world's great cities today, we think of New York, London, Tokyo, Rome, Sao Paulo, and others. But a city is coming in the future—an ancient city that has lain dormant for ages —that will dwarf today's world-class cities in opulence, commerce, finance, and sin.

I. **The Reasons for the Destruction of Babylon**
   A. Babylon Is Judged Because of Her Sorceries
   B. Babylon Is Judged Because of Her Seductions
   C. Babylon Is Judged Because of Her Sins
   D. Babylon Is Judged Because of Her Self-Glorification
   E. Babylon Is Judged Because of Her Slavery
   F. Babylon Is Judged Because of Her Sacrifices

II. **The Reactions to the Destruction of Babylon**
   A. The Monarchs of the Earth Will Mourn
   B. The Merchants of the Earth Will Mourn
   C. The Mariners of the Earth Will Mourn

III. **The Rejoicing in Heaven over the Destruction of Babylon**

IV. **Our Response to the Destruction of Babylon**

OVERVIEW

Beginning in 1926, a man named George S. Clason wrote a series of pamphlets on principles of financial management, supposedly drawn from the wisdom of ancient Babylon, the world's original seat of commerce and finance. The pamphlets were eventually published in book form, *The Richest Man in Babylon*. What Clason couldn't have known then is that Babylon is still alive and will again be the capital of commerce in the world.

According to Revelation 18, Babylon will be rebuilt and will be the commercial capital of the world during the Tribulation. The late Dr. Henry Morris, a scientist and geologist, wrote in his commentary on Revelation that Babylon is located at the geographical center of the world's land masses—an ideal spot for a world center of commerce. He quotes the eminent historian, Arnold Toynbee who agreed: Babylon is the best place in the world to build a world cultural metropolis because of its location at the crossroads of Europe, Asia, and Africa.[1]

The United States believes in the importance of this region. In 2009 the U. S. opened the largest embassy in the world in Baghdad: 27 buildings on 104 acres on the banks of the Tigris River. Long before modern experts identified the importance of Babylon, the prophets of old foresaw its importance in end-times prophecy.

Babylon's modern story begins with Iraq's former dictator, Saddam Hussein. He saw himself as a modern-day Nebuchadnezzar II, the king of Babylon in its original glory. Hussein invested more than $500 million in rebuilding ancient Babylon. He even had bricks inscribed with his name and the record of his acts, just as Nebuchadnezzar had done, and gold coins minted with his and Nebuchadnezzar's image. Obviously, Saddam Hussein's reign was cut short. But UNESCO (the United Nations Educational, Scientific, and Cultural Organization) is continuing the effort to turn ancient Babylon into a modern center for tourism and commerce.

Babylon is 60 miles south of modern Baghdad and was originally founded by Nimrod, the first world-level leader, if not dictator, responsible for the Tower of Babel (Genesis 10:8-10). According to Revelation, the Antichrist will be active in three cities: Rome (politics), Jerusalem (religion), and Babylon (commerce). Next to Jerusalem, Babylon is mentioned more than any other city in Scripture—and always in negative terms.

Both Jeremiah (51:26, 37, 43) and Isaiah (13:9, 19-20) prophesied that Babylon would one day become a desolate ruin. The fact is that those prophecies have never been totally fulfilled. Babylon is certainly not desolate today. Babylon changed hands from the Babylonians to the Medo-Persians to the Greeks and was never demolished throughout ancient history. So we know that the prophecy of Babylon's destruction is yet to be fulfilled, which means it must regain its glory.

Revelation 18 is an entire chapter devoted to the role and ruin of Babylon in the end times. We must remember that in Scripture Babylon represents more than a city—it is a metaphor for a greedy, corrupt world system dominated by man apart from God. From the days of the Tower of Babel to its role in the end of the world when the Antichrist controls world commerce from Babylon, it represents the rise and fall of man separated from God. Babylon represents humanism and rebellion from God, not just in one city but in the world system at large. Babylon stands for the world as we know it today: humanistic, proud, and increasingly detached from God as we near the end of the age.

THE REASONS FOR THE DESTRUCTION OF BABYLON (REVELATION 18:1-8)

Verses 1-2 picture the destruction of Babylon: "Babylon the great is fallen . . . !" The language John used illustrates an instantaneous action, not a gradual decline. Three times in this chapter we are told it will happen in one hour (verses 10, 17, 19). A world system on which people have built their whole lives will be gone in an hour.

There are three reasons God pours out His judgment on Babylon.

Babylon Is Judged Because of Her Sorceries
(Revelation 18:1-2)

John says Babylon "has become a dwelling place of demons, a prison for every foul spirit" (verse 2). The city will be a center of demonic activity, of depraved men and women seeking to advance their status in the world through commerce. Associated with demonic activity is the word "sorcery"—Greek *pharmaki* from which our word pharmacy (drugs) is derived. There will no doubt be unlimited use of drugs in Babylon as part of her depraved lifestyle.

Babylon Is Judged Because of Her Seductions (Revelation 18:3)

The nations and kings of the earth "have committed fornication with [Babylon], and the merchants of the earth have become rich through the abundance of her luxury." Babylon will one day be the richest, most liberated city on earth, home to every fleshly pleasure and pursuit. Immorality will replace morality in Babylon. The world will flock to Babylon to partake of her pleasures. Wealth will be multiplied for those who drink of Babylon's cup.

Wealth is on Babylon's horizon with Iraq having the third largest proven oil reserves in the world. But today she is the thirteenth largest producer of oil, meaning that Iraq's wealth is yet to be tapped and exploited. That will happen in Babylon's revival. John Phillips, in his commentary on Revelation, suggests that the world's crime syndicates will relocate to Babylon to go after their share of the wealth that will soon be flowing in Babylon.[2] Everyone in the world with an evil thought will be seduced and intoxicated by the lure of Babylon.

Babylon Is Judged Because of Her Sins (Revelation 18:5-6)

Verse 5 says that Babylon's "sins have reached to heaven, and God has remembered her iniquities." The word "reached" meant, in the original Greek, to be glued or stuck together, picturing Babylon's sins as having been joined together like bricks, piled on top of one another like bricks in a building. The image could not be more reminiscent of the Tower of Babel. God looks at modern Babylon's sins the same way He looked at ancient Babel's. Only this time the "building" has reached all the way to heaven as an affront to a holy God. Just as God judged Babel for her sins, He will judge Babylon for hers—indeed, a double portion of judgment (verse 6).

Babylon Is Judged Because of Her Self-Glorification (Revelation 18:7)

Babylon will position herself as a "queen" who "will not see sorrow"—a prideful, self-appointed position. She prophesies about herself that she will not see sorrow—that she will not be destroyed; that she is impregnable and invulnerable to outside forces; that she is the ultimate manifestation of the power of man in the world. This is certainly the pride of Nebuchadnezzar manifested again (Daniel 4:28-30).

Babylon Is Judged Because of Her Slavery (Revelation 18:12-13)

Verses 12-13 are an inventory of the kinds of merchandise that will be found in Babylon—28 categories of goods in all, with gold and silver topping the list. This list is set in terms familiar to the ancient world: woods, metals, spices, condiments, livestock, and others. But at the end of the list is something unexpected: "bodies and souls of men," indicating trafficking in human beings for slavery of various sorts to include, no doubt, sexual slaves. Every kind of sexual debauchery known to man will be present in Babylon. It is estimated that more than 27 million people are trapped in sexual slavery in the world today.[3] And God will judge Babylon for abusing precious human beings in such a perverted way.

Babylon Is Judged Because of Her Sacrifices (Revelation 18:24)

Found in Babylon will be "the blood of prophets and saints, and of all who were slain on the earth." In a city devoted to man, there will live some people who are devoted to God. But they won't live long. They will be martyred for their faith in a city that is anti-Christ. Remember: if true Christians do not submit to wearing the mark of the beast, they will stand out conspicuously in Babylon and will be killed for their rebellion against the Antichrist and his system.

So, Babylon will be judged for many things: sorceries, seductions, sins, self-glorification, slavery, and the sacrifices of God's people. Her destruction is summarized in verses 8-10—a day of "death and mourning and famine. And she will be utterly burned with fire, for strong is the Lord God who judges her" (verse 8). That which man thinks is indestructible will all be destroyed in one hour of one day. Six times in verses 21-23 the word "anymore" is used, as in everything that once was Babylon will not be found "anymore" —no music, no money, no majesty, no merchants, no monarchs, no merriment, no morality of man. All of it will be gone.

The destruction of Babylon will cause reactions from kings and nations around the globe.

THE REACTIONS TO THE DESTRUCTION OF BABYLON (REVELATION 18:9-19)

Two words are used to describe the reaction of the kings of the earth to Babylon's destruction: "Alas, alas!" In today's language, it would be like shaking one's head while moaning, "No, oh no! This can't be!" But it will be—a shock to those who viewed Babylon as untouchable.

The Monarchs of the Earth Will Mourn
(Revelation 18:9-10)

"The kings of the earth who committed fornication and lived luxuriously with her will weep and lament for her, when they see the smoke of her burning" (verse 9). The kings of the earth will have treated Babylon like a harlot, using the great city as a source of pleasure and diversion. They were tied to her in body, mind, and spirit, partaking of her luxuries in an ongoing life of wanton pleasure. Suddenly, the source of their wealth and pleasure will be reduced to a smoking heap, as were Sodom and Gomorrah. The kings of the earth will weep and mourn for their loss.

The Merchants of the Earth Will Mourn
(Revelation 18:11-17a)

All the merchandise we saw earlier? All gone. Babylon is no longer the great mall for the world's merchandise that she was: "And the merchants of the earth will weep and mourn over her" (verse 11). Why? Because "in one hour such great riches came to nothing" (verse 17). The economic hub of the world—the gravy train for the merchants of the world—has been destroyed. The entire world will be thrown into economic and financial chaos because of the destruction of Babylon.

Psalm 52:7 says, "Here is the man who did not make God his strength, but trusted in the abundance of his riches, and strengthened himself in his wickedness." A perfect description of the mourning merchants of the end-time world when the source of their wealth is destroyed.

The Mariners of the Earth Will Mourn
(Revelation 18:17b-19)

Revelation 18 verses 17b-19 show the trickle-down effect of the destruction of Babylon. The sea captains, piloting giant cargo ships around the globe, have suddenly lost their most profitable source of revenue: transporting goods to and from Babylon. During the Tribulation, the Persian Gulf will be flooded with merchant ships coming and going from Babylon, the great center of world commerce. There will no doubt be many in port on the day of Babylon's destruction, and many more coming and going in the waters of the Gulf. When they see the cloud of Babylon's destruction, they will weep and mourn over their loss.

But, if there is weeping on earth over Babylon's fall, there will be rejoicing in heaven.

THE REJOICING IN HEAVEN OVER THE DESTRUCTION OF BABYLON (REVELATION 18:20)

Verse 20 is an interesting parenthesis, an interlude, a snapshot of heaven's response to Babylon's fall: "Rejoice over her, O heaven, and you holy apostles and prophets, for God has avenged you on her!" This is a reference to what we have already seen in verse 24: the blood of prophets and saints who were killed in Babylon for their witness to Christ.

Monarchs, merchants, and mariners are mourning on earth while apostles, prophets, and saints are rejoicing in heaven! They rejoice over the destruction of a system that killed them, a system that set itself up in open rebellion against God. It was the spirit of Babylon that had been persecuting the martyrs of the church for 2,000 years. Saints who died in obscurity are now remembered in heaven as the system that killed them is brought to account. They had been waiting in heaven for justice, crying out, "How long, O Lord?" (Revelation 6:9-11) And justice has now been served.

Those who dispensed wrath upon the people of God will one day feel His wrath themselves. The words of Deuteronomy 32:35, quoted by Paul in Romans 12:19, are fulfilled: "'Vengeance is Mine, I will repay,' says the Lord." No wonder there is rejoicing in heaven! The rejoicing is not over the death of lost souls but over the establishment of righteousness and justice. The righteous arm of the Lord requites those whose lives were taken by the sinful acts of men.

OUR RESPONSE TO THE DESTRUCTION OF BABYLON (REVELATION 18:4)

One last verse supplies the application for Christians today who study the future revival and downfall of Babylon: "Come out of her my people, lest you share in her sins, and lest you receive of her plagues" (verse 4).

"My people" is a key phrase—God is speaking to Christians who are His people today. We are surrounded today by the spirit of

Babylon, the culture which will find its consummation in the Babylon of the future. And there is one message for us: Come out and be separate from the spirit and the city of Babylon.

There will be Christians living in Babylon at the time of her revival as a world city. Dr. Henry Morris has speculated on why there happens to be Christians in Babylon in the end times:

> Apparently, the same worldly allure will attract many believers to the final stage of Babylonian apostasy. The appeal of salary and prestige will entice many capable Christian business and professional men, architects, engineers, merchants, doctors, accountants, and others to participate in the planning and activation of this exciting and dynamic new metropolis. Christian workers in many construction and other trades will follow the enticement of high wages. No doubt, many of these Christians will rationalize their move to Babylon by the opportunity that will afford them to have a witness in the world's most important city, to the world's most important people.[4]

The danger in such a choice is obvious: getting caught up in the spirit and sin of Babylon. And thus God's plea to "Come out!" Seven times in the Bible there is an exhortation to God's people to "come out" of Babylon. God is always warning His people against sharing in the sins, and thus the judgments, of the world. You may not be living in the city of Babylon today; but if you are partaking in her spirit, today is the day to come out.

Notes:

1. Henry M. Morris, *The Revelation Record* (Wheaton, IL: Tyndale House, 1983), 348-349.

2. John Phillips, *Exploring Revelation—An Expository Commentary* (Grand Rapids: Kregel Publications 2001), 222.

3. Kevin Bales, *Disposable People: New Slavery in the Global Economy* (University of California Press, 1999) passim and product description at Amazon.com.< http://www.amazon.com? Disposable-People-Slavery-Global-Economy/dp/0520224639> (accessed 10 November 2009) and FreetheSlaves.net.

4. Ibid; Morris, 357.

1. Read Daniel 4:28-37.

   a. How did Nebuchadnezzar, king of Babylon, describe the city over which he reigned as king of Babylonia? (verse 30)

   b. For whose glory was Babylon built? (verse 30)

   c. What was God's overall response to Nebuchadnezzar's self-glorification? (verses 31-32) How does it parallel the response you have studied in Revelation 18?

   d. What was the first thing God told the king about his authority? (verse 31) How does this verify the words of Daniel spoken earlier in Daniel 2:21a?

   e. How would you describe the judgment issued to Nebuchadnezzar in verse 32a?

   f. How long would he remain in this condition? (verse 32b)

g. How was Nebuchadnezzar's punishment designed to teach him? (verse 32b)

h. How was the judgment fulfilled? (verse 33)

i. What did Nebuchadnezzar do at the end of the "seven times"? (verse 34)

j. What lessons about God did Nebuchadnezzar learn and proclaim? (verses 34-35)

k. What happened to Nebuchadnezzar after his disciplinary experience? (verse 36)

l. What newfound perspective did he bring to his role as king? (verse 37)

m. How does the last line of verse 37 correlate with James 4:6?

n. What lesson is there in Nebuchadnezzar's experience about intruding into the domain of God's glory?

2. In Jeremiah 51:26, how is the ultimate destiny of Babylon described?

   a. How does "desolate forever" indicate that Babylon still has a life? (Is Babylon "desolate" today?)

   b. How does verse 43 indicate that we have not yet seen the final days of Babylon?

3. Psalm 52 is about the wicked and the righteous.

   a. How do verses 1-5 fit the character of Babylon as described throughout Scripture and Revelation 18?

   b. How is the character of the righteous man different? (verses 6-9)

c. How does this dichotomy illustrate the need for God's people to "come out" of Babylon before getting trapped?

4. How is Proverbs 6:27 a warning to those who think they can live in Babylon without becoming defiled?

DID YOU KNOW?

The Hanging Gardens of Babylon are one of the Seven Wonders of the Ancient World. They were built by Nebuchadnezzar II, the king of Babylon mentioned in the Book of Daniel, around 600 B.C. They were a gift for the king's Persian wife who was homesick for the forests and lush vegetation of her homeland. The gardens were not so much "hanging" as "elevated" on platforms above the ground, high above the city floor. The Greek historian Strabo describes a screw-like device used to transport water into the gardens from below. The gardens are thought to have been destroyed in the second century B.C. by earthquakes.

GOD'S ULTIMATE NEW WORLD ORDER

Revelation 20:1-20

*In this lesson we get an overview of the Millennium—
the establishing of the kingdom of God on earth.*

OUTLINE

Writers, dreamers, and futurists through the ages have described
"golden ages" and "utopias" of various sorts, all to be brought about
by the upward evolution of man to a perfect state. The only true
golden age, God's Millennium, will be brought about in spite of man,
not because of him.

I. Five Purposes for God's Ultimate World Order
   A. To Remove Satan From the Earth
   B. To Reward the People of God
   C. To Respond to the Prophets' Predictions
   D. To Receive the Answer to the Disciples' Prayer
   E. To Reveal the Rebellion in the Heart of Man

II. Five Pictures of God's Ultimate World Order
   A. It Will Be a Time of Peace
   B. It Will Be a Time of Prosperity
   C. It Will Be a Time of Purity
   D. It Will Be a Time of Prolonged Life
   E. It Will Be a Time of Personal Joy

For the first time since I have lived there, California issued I.O.U.'s to citizens instead of the 2009 tax refunds they were due. And then they raised the state income tax rate (without asking us, I might add). The state of California, along with the federal government, is essentially "broke"—or at least in an illiquid state with debts far exceeding income.

We are so used to modern budgetary policies at the state and national levels that we forget how all of that is about to change. For instance, the vast majority of federal expenditures are for military and Medicare/Medicaid. But in God's coming new world order, there will be no wars (Isaiah 2:4) and no needy, sick, or poor persons (Psalm 72:2, 4, 12-14; Isaiah 11:4; 33:24; 35:5-6)! Imagine the difference that would make in a federal budget—and in our taxes. The Millennium will be a time of peace when King Jesus will meet the needs of those in His kingdom.

God's new world order, the Millennium, is presented to us in Revelation 20. "Millennium" means "a thousand years"—mentioned six times in Revelation 20:2-7. While the thousand years is specifically mentioned only here, God's kingdom age is mentioned throughout Scripture. In fact, Dr. J. Dwight Pentecost, one of the foremost authorities on prophecy in the Bible, says there is more information about the Millennium in the Bible than any other subject.[1]

The Millennium is preceded by the worst seven years in earth's history, the Tribulation. That is a period of judgment and separation, when those on earth who reject Christ are judged, leaving only believers (those who have become Christians during the Tribulation) to enter the Millennium—along with the saints of all previous ages who have been safe in heaven during the Tribulation. Christians who are raptured before the Tribulation return with Christ at His Second Coming to populate the Millennium along with saints from the Tribulation period. Seven bad years followed by one thousand glorious years is wonderful news! Jesus Christ will rule and reign for ten centuries with justice and peace over all the earth.

FIVE PURPOSES FOR GOD'S ULTIMATE WORLD ORDER

There are five prominent reasons for God's establishing a thousand-year reign of peace on earth.

To Remove Satan From the Earth
(Revelation 20:2-3)

The first thing that happens at the beginning of the Millennium is that Satan is removed from the earth. He is cast into "the bottomless pit . . . so that he should deceive the nations no more" for a thousand years. Satan is not destroyed—he is simply locked away so his influence in the world will not be felt. That alone will make an amazing difference in the nature of life on planet earth!

There will still be sin in the Millennium. Those who come into the Millennium from the Tribulation will still be human beings with a sin nature. They will have children and populate the earth with 25 more generations (generation = 40 years) of fallen human beings for a thousand years. So the human sin nature will be alive and well on planet earth, but Satan will not be around to stir up that sin nature in rebellion against God. And Christ's righteous judgments will keep sin in check.

So evil will be present, but nobody will be able to say, "The devil made me do it"—he will be off limits to planet earth. No one will be able to blame Satan for their sinful choices or their rebellion against God.

To Reward the People of God
(Revelation 20:4b)

The Bible is filled with references to God's rewards for His people (Isaiah 40:10; Matthew 16:27; Colossians 3:24; Revelation 22:12). Part of the Christian's reward will be to return to earth with Christ to rule with Him during the Millennium.

I believe a lack of emphasis on rewards is directly linked to the lack of motivation many Christians feel for serving the Lord today. Some Christians mistakenly think the idea of rewards is an impure motivation—a "what's-in-it-for-me" kind of thing. But that is an erroneous view of rewards. Living and reigning with Christ for a thousand years (verse 4b) is one of the greatest expectations Christians can have for the future. The parable of the talents indicates there will be a reward for faithfulness in service (Matthew 25:21).

Unfortunately, church leaders have made service for Christ seem like a yoke, burden, or dreaded obligation ("Please teach children's Sunday school just for one year—then you're done!"). Service isn't punishment! We tend to view service for Christ like our daily jobs—

and most people can't wait to be rid of their daily work. But service for Christ is our life, not our job.

I believe our service for Christ in the Millennium (our assignment from King Jesus) will be based on our faithfulness in serving Him in this life. That puts our current service in a different light—it determines what we'll be doing for a thousand years in the future!

To Respond to the Prophets' Predictions

The Old Testament prophets wrote extensively about God's coming "golden age" when God would rule with justice over the earth. They didn't see the gap between Christ's first and second comings, but they definitely anticipated Messiah's righteous rule.

- Kings have not yet fallen down before Christ, the Messiah (Psalm 72:11).
- Christ has not ruled yet on the throne of His father David with unending government and peace, judgment and justice (Isaiah 9:6-7).
- Christ's dominion has never been from sea to sea (Zechariah 9:10).
- Christ has never ruled over the "house of Jacob" (Luke 1:32-33).

These and other important predictions by the prophets have not been fulfilled, and God's character as a promise keeper requires that they will be. The Millennium will be the period in which all prophetic expectations about the will and rule of God will be fulfilled. Why does there need to be an earthly kingdom?

One of my seminary professors, Dr. Charles Ryrie, made this excellent point about the necessity of an earthly kingdom:

> Because Christ must be triumphant in the same arena where He was seemingly defeated. His rejection by the rulers of this world was on this earth. His exultation must also be on this earth. And so it shall be when He comes . . . to rule this world in righteousness. He has waited long for His inheritance; soon He shall receive it.[2]

To Receive the Answer to the Disciples' Prayer

The prayer Jesus taught His disciples to pray contains these lines—which get repeated without the understanding they deserve: "Your kingdom come, Your will be done on earth as it is in heaven" (Matthew 6:10). There has never been a time when God's kingdom has come and His will has been done on earth just like it is in heaven. But that day is coming! The will of God will be carried out completely when God the Son rules and reigns for a thousand years.

There is no opposition to the will of God in heaven; His will is always fulfilled. And that will be true of earth one day, but only when Christ rules during the Millennium (a period when Satan is bound from opposing the will of God). If the Millennium never happens, then it would forever be a prayer of the Son that the Father did not answer—which cannot happen since Christ always prayed in concert with the Father's will.

To Reveal the Rebellion in the Heart of Man

We live in an age when man's environment is blamed for his shortcomings: poor parenting, not enough money or education, pollution, civil injustice—you name it. But the Millennium will be a perfect environment that will demonstrate that man's problems are due to His own sin nature and being separated from God. There will be no environmental factors to blame. Even Satan will no longer be an excuse!

I've already mentioned that generations of people with sin natures will be born into a perfect environment in the Millennium. And when they choose to sin, it will be clear that it is because of their nature, not their lack of nurture. Some people born in the Millennium will turn toward God and some will not. Those who do not repent will make their decisions on the basis of their own fallen nature. And thus they will be held completely responsible for their decision to reject the King of Kings and His rule.

The Bible gives us five different images of what life will be like in the Millennium, the kind of kingdom Jesus will institute.

FIVE PICTURES OF GOD'S ULTIMATE WORLD ORDER

God's ultimate world order will be the opposite of life as we know it on earth today: a thousand years of peace, prosperity, purity, prolonged life, and personal joy.

It Will Be a Time of Peace

There have been wars on planet earth my entire life. Since 1941, there's never been a period of complete peace on planet earth. But that will change during the Millennium—a time of universal peace.

- There will be an abundance of peace (Psalm 72:7).
- Nations will not make war against each other (Micah 4:3).
- The animal kingdom will live in peace; harmony will exist between man and the animal kingdom as it was in the Garden of Eden (Isaiah 11:6-9).

- Many verses speak to the absence of peace the world has experienced, the peace it has longed for (Isaiah 59:8; Luke 1:79).

[This] will be a time when war will be utterly unknown. Not a single armament plant will be operating, not a soldier or a sailor will be in uniform, no military camps will exist, and not one cent will be spent for armaments of war, not a single penny will be used for defense, much less for offensive warfare. Can you imagine such an age when all the nations shall be at perfect peace, and all the resources of the earth, formerly used to protect the nation, are now available for enjoyment, [and] all industry engaged in the manufacture of the articles of war now are making articles of peace?[3]

It Will Be a Time of Prosperity

Today we are used to news about unemployment, stagnant wages, rising prices, and outsourcing of jobs to other countries. All that bad news will vanish during the Millennium—it will be a time of unparalleled prosperity. The curse on planet earth (Genesis 3:17) resulting from man's rebellion against God will be lifted. That curse made labor difficult and tiresome, a never-ending competition with the soil to give up food and sustenance. Man has lived since then by the sweat of his brow.

But in the Millennium the earth will burst forth with productivity. The prophets described it using the terminology common to their day—primarily agricultural—but we can easily translate their words into terms befitting a future economy:

- The wilderness and wasteland shall bloom abundantly; there will be streams in the desert (Isaiah 35:1-2).

- Commerce and wealth will flow unimpeded between peoples and nations as riches flow into Jerusalem, the world's capital (Isaiah 60:11).

- Trees of the field will yield their fruit in abundance; storehouses and vats will overflow with harvests; rains will water the earth generously (Ezekiel 34:26b-27a; 36:29b-30, 34-35; Joel 2:23-25a, 26a).

One of my favorite images is from Amos 9:13: "'Behold, the days are coming,' says the LORD, 'when the plowman shall overtake the reaper, and the treader of grapes him who sows seed; the mountains shall drip with sweet wine, and all the hills shall flow with it.'" One man is collecting the current harvest and another man is coming behind him with a plow to put in new seeds. In modern terms, you'll be making a deposit from your business and there will be somebody right behind you to give you more money. Prosperity, indeed!

It Will Be a Time of Purity

Justice will be totally pure during the Millennium, meaning there will be no wrong convictions, no delayed trials and sentencing, no influencing of juries. Jesus Christ will be judge and jury. His complete knowledge will allow Him to judge promptly, accurately, and justly. Individuals will come before Him charged with a crime and their case will be handled on the spot.

Today, even when someone is caught in the act of a crime, his prosecution can drag on for months due to lawyers' maneuverings, technicalities, and overcrowded dockets. And sometimes they may be set free based on the violation of some procedural matter. None of that will take place in the Millennium. Justice will be served— quickly, impartially, and righteously.

- The earth will be filled with the knowledge of the Lord (Isaiah 11:9).
- The whole earth will have been waiting for this kind of justice to be revealed (Isaiah 25:9).
- Justice will be pure, no conflicting or competing ideologies (Zechariah 13:2).

When Jesus—the one who said, "I am the . . . truth" (John 14:6) — rules the earth, pure truth will be manifested at every level of society.

It Will Be a Time of Prolonged Life

Life spans will be radically affected during the Millennium:
- A person who is 100 years old will be considered young (Isaiah 65:20).
- There will be a rapid multiplication of the human race (Jeremiah 30:19b).

It appears that the life spans that were common between the Garden of Eden and the flood of Noah will return to planet earth. And the vision of life seen in Job 5:26 will be the norm: "You shall come to the grave at a full age, as a sheaf of grain ripens in its season." Death will be only at the end of a very long and healthy life.

It Will Be a Time of Personal Joy

This may be the hardest one to imagine: life in a world characterized by joy and fulfillment instead of worry and foreboding.

- God will multiply joy among the nations (Isaiah 9:3).
- The whole earth will break forth in singing (Isaiah 14:7).
- Tears will be wiped away (Isaiah 25:8-9).
- New songs will be sung (Isaiah 42:10-12).

Perhaps we experience a taste of that joy around Christmas each year; but in the Millennium, it will be that way every day. Joy will emanate from the throne of King Jesus and permeate the earth.

Men have dreamed of a "utopia" on earth for ages, and it will finally arrive—but not through the efforts of man. It will come when the Son of God is established on His rightful throne in Jerusalem to proclaim peace and justice for a thousand years. Your only chance to participate in the Millennium with Jesus is to embrace Him now, by faith, while you have the opportunity. There will be no second chances. If you haven't already, trust Him as your Lord and Savior. The Millennium is a thousand years you don't want to miss!

Notes:

1. J. Dwight Pentecost, *Things to Come* (Grand Rapids: Academie Books, 1958), 476.
2. Charles Ryrie, *Basic Theology* (Wheaton, IL: Victor Books, 1986), 511.
3. Adapted from Lehman Strauss, *God's Plan for the Future* (Grand Rapids: Zondervan, 1965), 167-68.

1. Read Isaiah 2:1-4.

   a. When will the vision of Isaiah take place? (verse 2)

   b. What is the "mountain of the Lord's house"? (verse 2; see Isaiah 24:23)

   c. What does "on top of the mountains" and "above the hills" signify? (verse 2; what kind of supremacy does elevation imply?)

   d. How will the nations of the earth view Mount Zion and the temple? (verse 2)

   e. Why will people from the nations want to go up to Mount Zion? (verse 3a)

   f. What will flow out of Zion and Jerusalem? (verse 3b)

g. What will the Lord do from His position on Zion? (verse 4a)

h. What will the Lord force the nations to do with their swords? (verse 4b)

i. What will happen to the institution of war? (verse 4b)

j. What does "anymore" signify? How long-lasting will the abolition of war be? (verse 4b)

k. Of what use will organizations like the United Nations be during the Millennium?

2. What will King Jesus do for the poor and needy during the Millennium? (Psalm 72:2-4, 12-14)

a. What do "the rod of His mouth" and "breath of His lips" signify in His dealings on behalf of the poor and needy? (Isaiah 11:4)

b. How will the sick respond to the presence of the King in the Millennium? (Isaiah 33:24; 35:5-6)

3. Read Genesis 3:17-19.

   a. Why was the ground cursed in the Garden of Eden? (verse 17a)

   b. What was the impact of the curse on Adam? (verses 17b, 19a)

   c. What would the land produce that would make it difficult for Adam to grow food? (verse 18a)

   d. What does "sweat of your face" represent to us today? Why should we not be surprised that making a living is difficult? (verse 19)

   e. How does Paul picture the whole creation in light of the curse of Genesis 3? (Romans 8:22-23)

4. Describe the beautiful image of the Millennium found in Zechariah 8:23.

5. To what aspect of the Millennium do you most look forward to and why?

DID YOU KNOW?

The word "utopia" comes fittingly from the combination of two Greek words: *ou* (not) and *topos* (place). Therefore, a "utopia" is "not a real place" but a fanciful, mythical, or allegorical idea of such a place. Most civilizations have traditions of a "Golden Age"—a time of peace and prosperity for the human race. In spite of its biblical base, the doctrine of the Millennium has been co-opted and misused by religious cults in their teaching—groups such as the Branch Davidians, the Heaven's Gate cult, Jehovah's Witnesses, the Lord's Resistance Army, Millerism, and others. The longing of the human heart for a taste of heaven is based on Ecclesiastes 3:11 which says God has put "eternity in [people's] hearts."

Keep Your Head in the Game and Your Hope in God

Selected Scriptures

In this lesson we review biblical principles for managing money in unpredictable economic times

---

OUTLINE

We often allow finances to coast until a crisis arises. Such a crisis has arisen! It is time for God's people to get their financial house in order as good stewards of the grace and provision of God. Our ability to weather economic storms tomorrow may depend on our preparation today.

I. **Keep Your Head in the Game**

II. **Keep Your House in Order**
   A. Take a Personal Inventory
   B. Minimize Your Indebtedness
   C. Manage Your Money

III. **Keep Your Heart in Your Faith**

IV. **Keep Your Hope in God**

OVERVIEW

Many people know Gatlinburg, Tennessee, as a popular mountain-town resort, the gateway to the Great Smoky Mountains National Park. But it's also the location of beautiful mountain chalets, one of which is a 16,512 square foot enclave nestled in the mountains at the end of a climbing, windy road. The three-story-tall living room is now a silent memorial to greed and the desire for riches at the expense of others. As of May 2010, the home was in foreclosure and scheduled to be auctioned.

It was the home of Dennis Bole—some have referred to him as a hillbilly version of convicted Wall Street swindler Bernard Madoff. Using two shell investment companies, Bolze stole around $20 million from clients in the United States and Europe, many of whom lost their life savings and are hoping to reclaim something—anything— from the man who defrauded them. Bolze traded in his colossal chalet for a concrete cell in prison. But his investors are left with nothing but regrets.

Bolze's investors thought their money was safe, that nothing as terrible as fraud could happen to them. But Proverbs 23:5 says that money can sprout wings and fly off into the sky like an eagle. Many have found that to be true in the last two years as the world economic crisis has caused savings and investments to shrink drastically. People who planned on retiring are faced with the prospect of years of additional work to make up for lost ground.

We don't need to rehearse the heartbreak that many have experienced. The economic recession has touched the majority of average Americans in some way, so we have all felt the pain. Our time would be better spent talking about the future—how to prepare for the economic instability that, I believe, is coming in the years ahead. Scripture speaks about knowing the "signs of the times" (1 Chronicles 12:32; Matthew 16:3). We need to be practical and wise, but we also need to be faithful—full of faith—to the God who is our true source of security. We need to know how to keep our head in the game and our hope in God—the topic for this final lesson in our series on the hidden costs of the new global economy.

God's approach to money is opposite of the approach of the world. Money is important, of course, but it is not the priority. Rather than building a solid financial foundation, God wants us to build a solid spiritual foundation first. The spiritual principles we embrace will dictate how we handle money, so it's important to get spiritual priorities in place first.

Proverbs 27:24 says that money is temporary, not forever. Storing up money is like putting it into a bag with holes, Haggai warned (Haggai 1:6). Paul warns us through his first letter to Timothy about the dangers of loving money (1 Timothy 6). And Jesus set the kingdom tone for handling money when He said to store up treasures in heaven, not on earth (Matthew 6:19-21). Jesus was drawing a distinction between what is permanent and what is temporary.

In his book *Just Walk Across the Room—Simple Steps Pointing People to Faith*, Bill Hybels illustrates the difference between what lasts and what doesn't:

I was sitting in a meeting one time when the speaker suddenly unfurled a roll of stickers in his hand. "There is something we must all understand," he said as he walked across the front of the room. Periodically, he would stop and put a red sticker on a tiny replica of a house, and a red sticker on a Hot Wheels car, and a red sticker on a dollhouse-sized desk that represented our vocational lives. "You may not be able to tell from where you're sitting, but each red sticker has a single word on it," he said. "The word is temporary. And these things I'm putting them on are all temporary. They will fade away, turning cartwheels like leaves in the wind when this world ends. If you are living for these things, then you are living a life of temporary pleasure, temporary satisfaction, and temporary fulfillment."

He continued walking around the room, now silent as he labeled everything in sight with red stickers. I watched his hands declare the fate of the best this world has to offer as those stickers made their way to the goods in front of us. Temporary. Temporary. Temporary. "There is only one thing in this room that is not temporary," he continued. "There is only one thing that you can take with you into the next world." He called someone up to join him on the stage, and he placed a blue sticker on her lapel. "When you get to the end of your life and take in your last breath," he said, "what do you want your life to have been about? . . . "

No earthly commodity is going to make it from this world into the next. Not land, not homes, not bank accounts, not titles, not achievements. Only souls. Friends, Jesus Christ taught that every human being would be resurrected to spend an eternity in community with God in heaven or in isolation from God in hell. And because Jesus understood these eternal realities and believed them to the core of His being, he focused His attention on the only entity that would extend into the next reality: people. I don't know what the final assessment of my earthly life will be once I am gone. But I know this much: my quest while I am here is to seek people out and point them toward faith in God. I've tried enough approaches in my five decades of living to know that to invest yourself in anything other than people is to settle for the pursuit of a lesser vision—that ugly ensnaring trap of the temporal.[1]

King Solomon certainly agreed with Pastor Hybels—he devoted an entire chapter of Ecclesiastes to the futility of money and greed:

- The more we have, the more we want (Ecclesiastes 5:10).
- The more we have, the more we spend (Ecclesiastes 5:11).
- The more we have, the more we worry (Ecclesiastes 5:12).
- The more we have, the more we lose (Ecclesiastes 5:13-14).
- The more we have, the more we leave behind (Ecclesiastes 5:14-17).

Then Solomon went on to say two things about money and God. First, the power to earn money comes from God (Ecclesiastes 5:18); and, second, the power to enjoy money also comes from God (Ecclesiastes 5:19-20). This advice comes, remember, from the wealthiest man in the history of the world. Moses had taught the Israelites a similar truth as they prepared to cross into a land flowing with milk and honey: "It is He who gives you power to get wealth" (Deuteronomy 8:18).

Because we live in a world with opposite priorities, we have to make a conscious effort to make God's priorities our priorities.

KEEP YOUR HEAD IN THE GAME

When one of my sons was a quarterback on his high school football team, he suffered a concussion in a game without knowing it. He kept playing, but couldn't remember the names of plays or what down it was. He was in the game, but his head was definitely out of the game. After the game he had no memory of anything that happened after he took the hard hit that caused the concussion. In retrospect, he shouldn't have continued playing due to the risk of further injury.

Many people are playing the financial game today but without their spiritual head in the game. Every moment they are in jeopardy of taking a financial hit that will take them completely out of the game.

They think there's nothing they can do about the world economic situation, so they have just disconnected, hoping for the best. That is definitely not biblical. We are exhorted over and over to be alert, sober, and watchful in all areas of life (Romans 13:11; 1 Thessalonians 5:6). Rather than tuning out, we should be paying more and more attention to the unfolding economic disorder around us.

Every situation in life requires knowledge of the truth: how things are versus how they are supposed to be. We can then take steps to try to turn reality toward the ideal.[2] I have had to do that in my life and encourage you to do the same. Read books, talk to people you respect, tie up loose ends financially that you've let slide. Now is not the time to be less than an excellent steward of what God has entrusted to you.

Keep Your House in Order

Here are three suggestions for how to "keep your head in the game."

Take a Personal Inventory

My wife and I have taken these words to heart in the last several months. We had to acknowledge that our lives have been so busy that we have not paid as careful attention to our own financial house as we should have. So with the help of some experts in the field, we sat down to figure out exactly where we stand. There were some surprises, but they revealed things we need to focus on now rather than discovering them after they become bigger problems in the future.

The point is this: We can't change what we don't know about. We have to pull back the curtain and look at every aspect of our finances in order to know how vulnerable we are and how we can become better stewards.

Minimize Your Indebtedness

The late newspaper humorist, Lewis Grizzard, wrote a column telling about a coworker who put all his bills in a hat, pulling them out and paying them until he ran out of money. He felt all his creditors at least had an equal chance of getting paid with that system. And if he ever got a letter demanding payment, he would write back threatening not to even put them in the hat![3]

A lot of people today must be following a similar strategy— consumer debt in America reached $2.45 trillion in March, 2010.[4] Many people are finding it difficult to pay off debts and are resorting to consumer credit just to pay the bills. While the Bible doesn't forbid debt (but see Romans 13:8), it certainly warns against its misuse (Proverbs 6:1-2; 11:15; 17:18; 20:16; 22:7; 27:13). Many churches (like the church I pastor) sponsor financial counseling programs such as Crown Ministries (www.crown.org). I strongly encourage every Christian to participate in opportunities like this to get a handle on debt God's way.

Manage Your Money

While the Bible doesn't give investment advice, it certainly contains principles for managing our money, among which are these:

1. The Desire Principle: Desire God above all else and don't try to serve two masters (Matthew 6:19, 21, 24).

2. The Discernment Principle: Learn the principle of contentment and honesty (Proverbs 30:8-9).

3. The Discussion Principle: Listen to wise counsel; don't act impulsively or foolishly (Proverbs 19:20; 11:14).

4. The Discipline Principle: Be faithful and deliberate; don't fall for get-rich-quick schemes (Proverbs 28:20, 22).

5. The Depreciation Principle: Don't invest in things that are temporary; invest in things that will last for eternity (Matthew 6:19-20).

6. The Due Diligence Principle: Do your homework; count the costs (Luke 14:28-29).

7. The Diversification Principle: As the saying goes, "Don't put all your eggs in one basket" (Ecclesiastes 11:2).

8. The Descendant Principle: Invest in the future—your family and your descendants (Proverbs 13:22; 2 Corinthians 12:14; 1 Timothy 5:8).

9. The Devotion Principle: Honor the Lord with everything you have and from the firstfruits of your labor (Proverbs 3:9-10; 2 Corinthians 9:7).

These principles are not all the Bible says about money, but they form a paradigm for how to think biblically and act as a good steward.

Keep Your Heart in Your Faith

The Book of Daniel is one of the most important prophetic books in the Bible. And while it does not address economics directly, it certainly addresses the matter of security—trusting God regardless of how perilous the situation. There is an underlying theme in Daniel: God is in control of world history. Any rough spot we might encounter along the way must be viewed against the backdrop of His sovereign plans and purposes for the world and for us.

People today are feeling weak and fearful, even sick, about the state of our present and future economy. Daniel himself was made physically weak after seeing the visions God showed him of the future (Daniel 7:15; 7:28; 9:27; 10:2-3, 8, 15-16). And it is from Daniel's response to what he saw that we can find lessons to strengthen ourselves.

Daniel knew there was no way to get through the coming days except to go through them! We have not been promised an exemption except from the coming Tribulation. We need to put our heart in our faith and trust God as we go forward. Whether it was Daniel and his friends being asked to violate their conscience by eating Babylonian foods, or being told not to worship any god except the image of Nebuchadnezzar, Daniel and his three friends found a path of faith through each dilemma. Daniel was not afraid to stand up to the kings of Babylon and pronounce God's judgment— whether from a vision or from handwriting on the wall of the palace. Even when thrown into a den of lions, Daniel remained faithful.

Daniel is a perfect example of how to keep our head in the game and our heart in our faith, walking uprightly and resolutely with faith in God. I encourage you to read and reread the book of Daniel as a way to strengthen your heart in these days.

Keep Your Hope in God

There's a saying I've seen on bumper stickers and on church marquees that says, "Know God, Know Hope. No God, No Hope." That is the central message of the 10 lessons in this study guide. Those who know God and walk with Him through life's ups and downs have hope. Those who don't know God can hope only in the unpredictable events of this world to dictate their future and their fate.

Life offers many reasons for discouragement these days, but the Bible offers many more reasons for hope! Nothing says it better than Psalm 42:5: "Why are you cast down, O my soul? And why are you disquieted within me? Hope in God, for I shall yet praise Him for the help of His countenance." We must take responsibility for the condition of our soul and remind ourselves—preach to ourselves!—to hope in God.

Hope in God turns to gladness (Proverbs 10:28) and makes us like an immovable tree (Jeremiah 17:7-8). Hope gives us the ability to wait and trust with quietness of soul (Lamentations 3:21-26). Whatever the future brings, if we know God, we know hope. I trust that you know Him today—that your hope in Him is your eternal shelter.

Notes:

1. Bill Hybels, *Just Walk Across the Room: Simple Steps Pointing People to Faith* (Grand Rapids, MI: Zondervan, 2006), 186-187.

2. Frank J. Hanna, *What Your Money Means and How to Use It Well* (New York: Crossroad Publishing Company, 2008), 7-8.

3. Quoted by Ron Blue and Jeremy White, *Surviving the Financial Meltdown*, (Wheaton, IL: Tyndale House Publishing, 2009), 38.

4. Federal Reserve Statistical Release, "G.19 Report on Consumer Credit," 07 May 2010, <http://www.federalreserve.gov/releases/g19/Current/> (accessed 10 May 2010).

APPLICATION

1. Read Luke 12:13-21.

   a. Read through this parable and see if you can discern what was probably the motivation of the man making the request in verse 13.

   b. It has been said that covetousness (verse 15) is broken every time any of the other Ten Commandments is broken. Why would this be true? (See Exodus 20:1-17.)

   c. How does Jesus' principle in Luke 15b apply to your life?

   d. What is suggested about the nature of greed by the man in the parable being identified as already "rich?" (verse 16)

   e. How rich is he? (verse 17)

   f. What might he have done with his many goods instead of the solution he settled on in verse 18?

   g. How did God force the man to share some of his abundance with others? (verse 20)

h. Compare verse 19 with Genesis 3:17-19. How accurate was the man's understanding of life in our world?

i. Based on verse 21, write your own definition of what it means to be rich.

j. Defend the position of your choice: "It is/is not possible to be rich in treasures and also rich toward God."

k. Based on your own definition of rich, how rich are you?

2. Describe the subtlety of covetousness in terms of Exodus 20:17 and Deuteronomy 5:21. That is, what is the difference between "seeing," "admiring," and "wanting" your neighbor's property (or something like it)?

3. Based on Job 31:24-25, why did Job come to the conclusion he reached in verse 28?

a. In what way is this idea similar to Jesus' words in Matthew 6:24?

b. What does it show about us if we fail to include God in all our financial decisions? What does it suggest about who we believe is the true owner of our money?

4. If you had the chance to ask the apostle Paul about the wisdom of incurring any kind of debt, what do you think he would say based on Romans 13:8? What was Paul communicating in that verse?

DID YOU KNOW?

Mentioned in this lesson are ministries such as Crown Financial Ministries that offer in-church classes and counselors to help believers apply biblical principles to family finances. In addition to Dr. Jeremiah's books and tapes, time-tested Christian authors such as (the late) Larry Burkett, Ron Blue, and Dave Ramsey offer books, tapes, and other resources that provide biblical stewardship principles. While Turning Point cannot provide blanket endorsements of these or other Christian authors and counselors, we do encourage you to seek out any and all resources that will help you achieve your goal of becoming a good steward of your finances. The days ahead may be some of the most strenuous this generation has faced, and we encourage you to follow the biblical principle of preparation by counting the cost (Luke 14:28).

ADDITIONAL RESOURCES
BY DR. DAVID JEREMIAH

The Handwriting on the Wall

Daniel, divinely inspired, accurately prophesied the rise and fall of empires and their rulers. We cannot pass Daniel off as just the man in the lion's den or the "dreamer." To know Daniel is to know how to live today and look into the future with confidence.

Escape the Coming Night

Let Dr. David Jeremiah be your guide through the terrifying heights and unfathomable depths of the Book of Revelation. Arm yourself with prophetic truth about things to come so you can live every moment for God in faith and confidence.

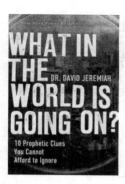

What in the World Is Going On?

Dr. David Jeremiah has faithfully taught the prophetic portions of Scripture for more than four decades. In this important book he shines the light of God's Word on the prophetic path now unfolding before the Church and the world by examining ten important clues through the lens of Scripture.

Living With Confidence in a Chaotic World

The times we are living in are troubling, but as Christians we do not need to live in fear. Dr. David Jeremiah takes you through ten biblical principles, each based squarely on the Truth of God's Word, to give you a roadmap to follow during these chaotic times. If your confidence is being eroded by world events, let *Living With Confidence in a Chaotic World—What on Earth Should We Do Now?* show you what to do to stay confident in Christ.

Each of these resources was created from a teaching series by Dr. David Jeremiah. Each series is available with correlating study guide and CD audio albums.

For pricing information and ordering, contact us at

P.O. Box 3838
San Diego, CA 92163
(800) 947-1993
www.DavidJeremiah.org

STAY CONNECTED
TO DR. DAVID JEREMIAH

Take advantage of two great ways to let Dr. David Jeremiah give you spiritual direction every day! Both are absolutely FREE!

Turning Points Magazine and Devotional

Receive Dr. David Jeremiah's monthly magazine, *Turning Points* each month:

- Monthly Study Focus
- 48 pages of life-changing reading
- Relevant Articles
- Special Features
- Humor Section
- Family Section
- Daily devotional readings for each day of the month
- Bible study resource offers
- Live Event Schedule
- Radio & Television Information

Your Daily Turning Point E-Devotional

Start your day off right! Find words of inspiration and spiritual motivation waiting for you on your computer every morning! You can receive a daily e-devotion communication from David Jeremiah that will strengthen your walk with God and encourage you to live the authentic Christian life.

Sign up for these two free services by visiting us online at www.DavidJeremiah.org and clicking on DEVOTIONALS to sign up for your monthly copy of *Turning Points* and your Daily Turning Point.